3B86

D0234382

OXFORD MEDICAL PUBLICATIONS

The consultation: an approach to learning and teaching

This book is to be returned on or before
the last date stamped below.

OXFORD GENERAL PRACTICE SERIES

Editorial Board

1. Paediatric problems in general practice
   M. Modell and R. H. Boyd
2. Geriatric problems in general practice
   G. Wilcock, J. A. M. Gray, and P. M. M. Pritchard
3. Preventive medicine in general practice
   edited by J. A. M. Gray and G. H. Fowler
4. Women's problems in general practice
   edited by A. McPherson and A. Anderson
5. Locomotor disability in general practice
   edited by M. I. V. Jayson and R. Million
6. The consultation: an approach to learning and teaching
   D. Pendleton, T. Schofield, P. Tate, and P. Havelock
7. Continuing care: the management of chronic disease
   edited by J. C. Hasler and T. P. C. Schofield
8. Management in general practice
   P. M. M. Pritchard, K. E. Low, and M. Whalen
9. Modern obstetrics in general practice
   edited by G. N. Marsh

The consultation: an approach to learning and teaching

Oxford General Practice Series 6

DAVID PENDLETON
Fellow, The King's Fund College, London

THEO SCHOFIELD
General Practitioner, Shipston-on-Stour and Associate Regional Adviser, Oxford

PETER TATE
General Practitioner and Course Organizer, Abingdon

PETER HAVELOCK
General Practitioner and Course Organizer, Wooburn Green, Buckinghamshire

OXFORD NEW YORK TORONTO MELBOURNE
OXFORD UNIVERSITY PRESS

Oxford University Press, Walton Street, Oxford OX2 6DP

Oxford New York Toronto
Dehli Bombay Calcutta Madras Karachi
Kuala Lumpur Singapore Hong Kong Tokyo
Nairobi Dar es Salaam Cape Town
Melbourne Auckland
and associated companies in
Beirut Berlin Ibadan Nicosia

Oxford is a trade mark of Oxford University Press

First published 1984
Reprinted 1984, 1985

British Library Cataloguing in Publication Data

The Consultation.—(Oxford general practice series ; 6)
1. Medical consultation—study and teaching
I. Pendleton, David
610.69'6   RC65
ISBN 0-19-261349-9

Library of Congress Cataloging in Publication Data

Main entry under title :
The Consultation.
(Oxford general practice series ; 6)
Bibliography: p.   Includes index.
1. Physician and patient—Study and teaching.
2. Physicians (General practice)   3. Medicine, Clinical
—Study and teaching.   I. Pendleton, David.   II. Series:
Oxford general practice series ; no. 6.
R727.3.C675   1983   610.69'6   83-19349
ISBN 0-19-261349-9 (pbk.)

Printed in Great Britain by
William Clowes Limited
Beccles and London

To Ben Pomryn

Foreword

John Horder
Former President, Royal College of General Practitioners
Visiting Fellow, King's Fund College

Patients sometimes go away from a consultation disappointed with the outcome.

They may, of course, have brought an insoluble problem. But supposing the problem which mattered to them was not even recognized? Byrne and Long (1976) found that a frequent reason for failure was because the doctor had not found out why the patient was there.

This book is about what doctors and patients can try to achieve in the consultation and why they succeed or fail. What happens in those few pregnant minutes behind closed doors needs to be thought about and understood.

We all know that people bring problems which cannot always be made into diseases, and that they will often bring several to one consultation. Even for one presented problem, a successful response calls for more than one sort of diagnosis. As Sir James Spence put it in 1960:

Before explanation and advice can be given to a patient, three diagnoses must be made – the diagnosis of the disease, of the concept or fears of the disease in the mind of the patient, and of the patient's capacity to understand the explanation.

This book stresses patients' concepts and fears – their beliefs. Only if the doctor listens closely and enters into the way in which they see things, and picks up the way in which they express themselves, will they be able to understand and co-operate. This is one important key to success or failure.

But it stresses something more. One consultation influences another. What happens today will influence what happens next time, even if no treatment has been offered. The patient's ideas about his problem, about his own health more generally, and about the doctor will have changed.

Patients' health beliefs and their attempts to understand their own health strongly influence their well-being and how they try to look after themselves. Thus, helping people to express their beliefs and to develop their understanding may not be optional extras in the consultation, to be dropped when time presses, as it usually does.

As in the consultation, so in the tutorial – what the student or trainee brings by way of understanding is the place to start, the foundation to be built upon. There are no *tabulae rasae*.

So, reader, if you are a clinician, this book asks to what uses are you putting your consultations. There are choices to be made. What are you actually trying

to do? And if you are also a teacher, what do your students or trainees expect
from the consultation when they start, and what new choices do you put before
them?

REFERENCES

Byrne, P.S. and Long, B.E.L. (1976). *Doctors talking to patients.* HMSO, London.
Spence, J. (1960). *The purpose and practice of medicine.* Oxford University Press.

Preface

This book has been written with the needs of several groups of people in mind. General practitioners have an interest in the consultation, both as practising doctors and as teachers. Social scientists also have an interest both in the behaviour in the consulting room and in measuring the effects of consultations on both doctor and patient alike.

All general practitioners have a vested interest in trying to practise as effectively as they know how, but many may be unsure how best to decide what is effective and what is not. This is even more of a problem for all those who are involved as teachers either at undergraduate (medical school) level or at post-graduate (vocational and continuing education) levels.

In this book we have tried to address the needs of all who are interested in the general practice consultation. The first two chapters provide a review of other approaches to the study and teaching on the subject of the consultation. A considerable amount of evidence is presented in these early chapters on which our approach is based. In Chapter 3 we provide a new model of the consultation which attempts to be comprehensive. This model is based on the events which surround a consultation, and from this we derive the tasks which may have to be achieved in order for a consultation to be considered effective. These tasks are described in detail in Chapter 4, whereas alternative methods for achieving the tasks are outlined in Chapter 5.

Chapter 6 describes our approach to learning and teaching and in Chapter 7 we discuss the various settings in which we have made use of these ideas. Chapter 8 provides practical help for those who are keen to observe real consultations. It describes the advantages and disadvantages of the methods in current use and suggests means whereby the use of recording techniques, both audio and video, might be used to good effect.

In Chapter 9 we consider the ethical issues which our work raises. We also outline the acceptability of the techniques used. In Chapter 10 we look critically at our own work and detail some of the main unresolved issues.

It should be clear from all this that a reader may not need to read the entire book in order to use it for his own purposes. Although this book is written as a whole, each chapter has a summary at the end so that any reader can browse through the main ideas in the book in a few minutes. The general practitioner who wants to use our approach to look at his own consultations may only wish to read Chapters 4–9. The researcher may only read Chapters 1–3 and Chapter 10. Anyone who wants to consider our definition of an effective consultation may only need to read Chapters 3 and 4. General practice teachers, on the other hand, might be encouraged to read the whole book, in order to understand the issues more fully.

Our approach has been put together over several years and has been the result of a lot of background reading, of research, and of medical practice. It is also well tried and tested in a variety of training groups. It is not the simplest of approaches and some may think this is a disadvantage. We have not tried to make it simple at all costs. We have attempted to put together an approach which is above all comprehensive and coherent. After that we have attempted to make it as simple as possible, but we have tried not to sacrifice the comprehensiveness for simplicity. We would argue that this is appropriate and that as complex an event as the general practice consultation will not be compressed into a few simple statements.

We recognize that this work would not have progressed, however, without the help and support of a large number of friends and colleagues. We should like to take this opportunity to thank some of them. We are grateful for the encouragement and willingness to experiment with these and earlier ideas of the course organizers, trainers, and trainees of the Oxford Region's Vocational Training Scheme in General Practice. We are especially grateful to Dr John Hasler, the Regional Adviser in General Practice who has always been our most loyal supporter and keenest critic. Many of the research ideas were developed with the help of the Department of Experimental Psychology of the University of Oxford. Our special thanks go to Dr Michael Argyle and Dr Jos Jaspars.

We also want to acknowledge those who have typed innumerable drafts of this work: Judith Goodman, Elizabeth Rouse, and Deborah Farrell. Judith Halliwell and Osborne also fought in vain to produce longer sentences.

Most of all, we must thank our wives, who supported our enthusiasm and tolerated our absences.

D.P., T.S.,
P.T., P.H.

Contents

1 General approaches to the consultation

The consultation is the central act of medicine, and as such it deserves to be understood. It has been estimated that on some days there are over a million general practice consultations in the United Kingdom alone. This book will describe an approach to the consultation in general practice, but many of the ideas are equally relevant to other branches of medicine. Each consultation may deal with matters of considerable consequence – any problem may be presented to a general practitioner, and he must make a response. Some consultations will deal with sore throats or holiday vaccinations; some problems may be resolved easily, and some will prove intractable or even impossible to resolve. To the patient the general practitioner is the first line of medical contact, and for the general practitioner the patients are at one and the same time the greatest source of job satisfaction and of frustration. To doctor and patient alike the general practice consultation is the medium through which medicine is most frequently practised.

Each consultation is part of a constantly changing pattern of events for doctor and patients. It has its antecedents, it processes, its consequences, and each has been the subject of scrutiny. In this chapter we shall review six previous approaches to the study of the consultation: the medical approach is primarily concerned with **diseases and diagnosis**. Sociology, anthropology, and transactional analysis, by contrast, deal with the **roles** played by doctor and patient. The approach made by Balint and others emphasizes the **dynamics** of the consultation, whereas social psychologists have been more concerned with the **behaviour** of doctor and patient. We shall describe each approach and consider its strengths, its limitations and its implications, in order that we may glean as much as possible from each. In so doing, we shall come to see the need for a more comprehensive understanding of the consultation than any or all of the approaches afford.

THE MEDICAL APPROACH TO THE CONSULTATION

The practice of modern medicine is based on two fundamental concepts, that of disease and that of diagnosis.

Disease

Since the Renaissance medical scientists have studied the normal structure and function of the body and the changes that can occur in 'disease'. Diseases have been defined or classified sometimes at the level of a clinical description of a syndrome, sometimes in terms of abnormalities of structure and function, but these descriptions have always been considered incomplete without the definition of the cause or aetiology. A classic example of the strength of this approach was the demonstration by Robert Koch in 1882 that the syndrome of consumption, which was known to be associated with the structural changes of cavitation in the lungs, was caused by the tubercle bacillus. He did this by satisfying strict postulates for the evidence required before a particular microbe could be regarded as the cause of a particular disease.

This rigorous scientific approach has been responsible for many of the achievements of modern technological medicine. The belief that every illness is caused by a disease which has an external definable cause is not, however, adequate in many situations. Even in such a defined condition as tuberculosis it does not explain variations in susceptibility, in the course of the illness, or in the degree of disability between different patients. In many other diseases no single external definable cause can be found. We have searched in vain, for example, for a single cause for ischaemic heart disease and now believe it to be due to a complex interaction between physical factors, such as blood pressure and serum lipids, social factors and lifestyle, and individual personality.

The alternative to the scientific approach has recently been termed 'holistic' but in fact can be traced back to the writings of Hippocrates. In this approach any problem is defined simultaneously in terms of its physical, psychological, and social components. The cause of the problem, the way it will be dealt with, and its progression are determined by the patient's understanding of and emotional response to what is hapenning. The patient's relationships and the effects of the problem on them are also important and all these, therefore, must form a fundamental part of the original definition of the problem.

Ian McWhinney (1981) has eloquently made the case that this holistic theory of disease should be recognized as the scientific basis of Family Medicine.

This is not a matter of rejecting the reductive (disease) theory, but enlarging its scope to overcome its limitations. The holistic approach recognises that illness is closely related to the personality and experience of the patient, and that man can not be understood in isolation from his environment. The holistic view acknowledges that every illness is different, and that the physician himself is an important aspect of the healing process.

Campbell, Scadding, and Roberts (1979) explored these differing concepts of disease between groups of medical and non-medical people. They were asked to indicate whether they thought a number of common diagnostic terms referred to a disease or not. All groups rated illness due to infection as disease, but doctors, particularly general practitioners, were more generous in accepting non-infectious conditions as diseases, for example, alcoholism, schizophrenia, or hypertension. To the laymen, a disease seems to imply a living agency that caused illness, but for both medical and non-medical people, apart from the nature of the cause, the most influential factor in determining whether or not an illness was thought to be a disease was the contribution of the doctor to its diagnosis and treatment.

There are important consequences of these beliefs. If patients believe that their illness is due to a disease which has an external cause then they can feel absolved of any responsibility for their own health. If the doctors share this belief then they in turn will be willing to take on this responsibility. Ivan Illich (1977) has questioned this process of the 'medicalization of health', and the effectiveness of the application of modern technological medicine to all life's problems. It is essential for doctors to distinguish between the recognition that all their patient's problems have psychological and social components and the decision to assume responsibility for these components. Helping patients to solve their own problems must be a fundamental therapeutic activity.

Similar considerations apply to the prevention of disease. The accurate definition of the cause has been the essential step in the prevention of many diseases, from cholera and the Broad Street pump* to lung cancer and cigarettes. For many diseases, however, the method has not been medical intervention but improved social conditions and for many of the other diseases which continue, for example lung cancer, the key will lie with changes in individuals' understanding and behaviour.

Diagnosis

It is generally considered to be axiomatic that the essential first step in any consultation with a patient is to make an accurate diagnosis. Without a diagnosis the doctor is unable to make a prediction about the future course of the patient's problem or to plan its management.

This axiom is equally true for general practice. The difficulties come, however, in deciding what should be included in a diagnosis and the methods that can be used to achieve it.

The traditional medical diagnosis would always include a definition of the cause of the patient's problem, as this will allow the possibility of 'rational' treatment directed at the cause, as well as making predictions about the prognosis more reliable. We have already argued, however, that a statement of the cause of many of the problems seen in general practice must include environmental, social, and psychological factors, as well as physical ones. One of our difficulties is our continued lack of adequate classification, definition, and terminology for these factors. McWhinney (1972) in his article 'Beyond diagnosis' proposed a taxonomy of social factors in illness with seven categories: loss, conflict, change, maladjustment, stress, isolation, and failure. Psychological factors on the other hand are usually defined in terms taken from formal

---

*During the 1854 epidemic of cholera over 500 deaths occurred in ten days in a small area of central London. John Snow, an anaesthetist and epidemiologist, showed that only those who obtained their drinking water from the Broad Street pump had contracted cholera. He advised removing the pump handle and a few days after this was done no new cases were reported.

psychiatry, such as anxiety and depression, which can in turn lead to a false sense of understanding of their cause and prognosis and to inappropriate management.

Another dimension of diagnosis in general practice that will be considered in more detail in subsequent chapters is defining not only the nature and cause of the patient's problem, but also the reasons why the patient has presented at that particular time and what the patient's own ideas, concerns, and expectations about the problem are. Balint (1957) emphasized the need for general practitioners to be able to make a 'deeper diagnosis and develop a more comprehensive understanding of the patient's concern and behaviour'. Browne and Freeling (1976) also described this special function of the general practitioner as

to understand the whole of his patient's communication, so that he could assess the whole person and be able to consider the effect of any intervention in an illness on the whole life of his patient.

The problem facing a general practitioner is to decide how deep and how comprehensive a diagnosis is required at any particular time. The medical definition of a diagnosis as 'a statement of the nature and cause of the patient's problem sufficient to make an accurate prognosis and plan rational treatment' must continue to be the basis of good medical practice.

The diagnostic process

The classical medical diagnostic process consists of a sequence of history taking, physical examination, and laboratory investigation, with the history taking and physical examination following a set, comprehensive routine and the diagnosis being formulated only at the conclusion of the process. Hampton, Harrison, Mitchell, Pritchard, and Seymour (1975) looked at the relative contributions of these three phases to diagnosis and management of medical out-patients and showed that the diagnosis that agreed with the final diagnosis could have been made after taking the history alone in 66 of the 80 patients studied. The physical examination was only useful with seven patients and the laboratory investigations with a further seven. Other studies, notably the work of Elstein, Shulman, and Sprafha (1978), have shown that clinicians both in hospital and in family practice do not normally operate in this way, but generate hypotheses early in the consultation and direct the consultation towards testing these hypotheses in turn. This will be discussed fully in Chapter 5.

Not only is the classical medical model of the consultation inaccurate, it is also an incomplete description and omits such areas as the exploration of the patient's ideas, the use of non-verbal communication, the therapeutic use of the doctor–patient relationship and the giving of explanations. These omissions and their implications for teaching will be discussed in subsequent sections of the book.

Another dimension that is omitted from the classical model is that a consultation can be one of a series. This is particularly true of the consultation in general practice, but is also applicable in other disciplines. Stott and Davis (1979) described a four-part framework to describe the exceptional potential in each primary care consultation. This four part framework is described in Table 1.1.

Table 1.1. *The potential of each primary care consultation (Stott and Davis 1979)*

A Management of presenting problems	B Modification of help-seeking behaviours
C Management of continuing problems	D Opportunistic health promotion

The relevance of this framework for the consultation will be discussed in Chapter 4.

SUMMARY

The challenge facing general practitioners is to apply the scientific discipline of the medical model while at the same time broadening the concept of disease and illness, making more comprehensive diagnoses and developing diagnostic techniques appropriate to the wide variety of patients and problems presented to them as doctors.

THE SOCIOLOGICAL APPROACH TO THE CONSULTATION*

The approach that sociology makes to the consultation is to seek to understand the behaviour not between a doctor and a patient, but rather between 'doctors' and 'patients'. It seeks to identify social factors that can be shown to influence and predict behaviour in the consultation. These **social factors** are defined as significant elements of behaviour and belief that are shared by members of a group, in this case doctors and patients.

Two significant social factors that are thought to govern social action are **values and norms**. Values refer to shared beliefs and are conceived of at a relatively abstract level, while norms, on the other hand, are more concrete ways of feeling, thinking, and acting that reflect a set of beliefs. Norms and values are learnt from other members of ones social group, and are maintained by the process of social control.

*Much of this section is based on the work of David Tuckett, *An introduction to medical sociology* (1976), to which readers are referred for a much fuller discussion.

For example, many groups value truth and honesty, but while all members of the social group may share this value they may not always behave honestly. The group, however, discourages dishonesty, both by informal processes, such as ostracism, or by formal processes such as law enforcement and the Courts. Honesty is a value possessed by most groups and in the consultation we can usually make the assumption that it is shared by the other person.

There are many other values and norms, however, that are not necessarily shared. For example, while the doctor may have invested in his long-term future with a 25-year mortgage and a contributory pension, his working class patient may be budgeting from week to week. This difference in perspective may be one factor to explain why some working-class patients fail to conform with such measures as giving up smoking or attending antenatal clinics which appear eminently sensible to their doctors.

Doctors acquire norms and values, not only from their family and social background, but also from their training. An individual entering medical school, or indeed general practice, is sensitive to the particular values and norms that exist in a new setting and gradually adapts so that he comes to think as, act as, and indeed 'is a doctor'. Sociologists have analysed what 'being a doctor' means by looking at the relationship between the individual and the **role** that he plays. This is not to say that doctors acting out a role are not genuine, but rather that this approach identifies the common features, behaviours, and rules involved in playing a particular role.

There is also a role 'patient', which has its own, but different rules. In the consultation both may see that the doctor's role is to ask questions, the patient's role is to provide answers and that playing these roles determines the behaviour in the consultation. Boreham and Gibson (1978) showed that both doctors and patients saw this sort of behaviour as 'good'. If, on the other hand, behaviour is to be different, with the patients asking questions and the doctor providing answers, then both parties will need to have a different view of their roles.

Social factors not only affect the consultation itself, but also its antecedents and outcomes. Patients from various social classes with their associated differences in employment, economic status, housing, and education, have widely divergent experiences of health. These inequalities were described and discussed in detail in the Black Report, *Inequalities in health* (1980). The relationship between some of these factors and particular diseases is sometimes not fully understood, but in other cases the links are well established. Brown and Harris (1978), studying the onset of depression in a group of women between the ages of 18 and 65, found that a combination of life crises, such as bereavement, job losses, marital separation, and moving house, and longer-term difficulties, such as bad housing or severe economic deprivation, could account for the large majority of the depressive episodes in their study group.

There is considerable evidence (reviewed by Tuckett 1976) that:

Individuals have symptoms much of the time, and that dealing with them, particularly by self-medication, is a day-to-day activity: that individuals visit the doctor on average for only one of about 10 symptoms that they suffer: that when they do go these symptoms have not necessarily got worse: that their motives for going and what they want from the doctor, may often have more to do with some change in their social circumstances than with any change in symptoms.

A wide variety of social and cultural factors have been identified as influencing the decision to seek medical help. Tuckett argues that, in the United Kingdom at least, the large majority of individuals have previous experience of consulting a doctor as a patient and that this experience influences the patient's expectations and the potential value of deciding to seek help from a doctor. This value may include help to solve the presenting problem, but also other benefits which are more general. Labelling the problems as illness may absolve the patient from some responsibilities, for example, employment, and legitimize a person's behaviour and demands for care. On the other hand there may be costs in the decision to seek help – it may involve increased dependence, particularly on the doctor, increased uncertainty, stigma, and sometimes financial loss.

To the extent that **illness** is defined as an abnormal state by society or a social group, it becomes regarded as deviant and medicine has an important role in social control. It acts to define and legitimize what is illness and what is not, and it has the task of managing and returning to their former 'healthy status' those who become defined as 'ill'. There is a danger, however, that many of the problems defined as 'illness' are merely 'problems of living'. To label them as 'illness' diverts attention from very real social problems that need to be faced, rather than to be seen as illnesses and swept under the carpet by 'treatment'. Depression through social causes has already been discussed and is a good example of this process. While antidepressant medication may alleviate many of the symptoms, it will do little for unemployment, bad housing, and social isolation which may be the cause of the depression.

Social factors can also affect the outcome of consultations. Any management plan agreed in the consultation has to be applied by the individual in his social setting. In addition, the way that doctors and patients judge whether a particular outcome is successful is dependent on their norms and values. Tuckett (1976) gives the example of a man who has a leg amputated and describes the alternative outcomes that may be given quite different priorities by different people, depending on their role and their values. This is illustrated in Table 1.2

Table 1.2. *Possible outcomes (Tuckett 1976)*

Initial intervention	Outcomes
Amputation	The operation scar has healed well and the patient can leave hospital
	The cancer seems to be spreading to the rest of the body
	He uses a wheelchair in preference to his artificial leg
	He has lost his former job and is now unemployed
	His wife, disappointed at being married to a 'cripple' has left him

Sociology can be criticized as a science based on making generalizations about groups, and it can be argued, therefore, that the information is of little help in understanding the behaviour of the individual. In this respect, however, it does not differ from the majority of probability statements made in other medical sciences that we accept as a basis for action – for example, when we embark on treating a man with a raised blood pressure, we do not know that without treatment he will certainly suffer a stroke, but only that he is more likely to do so.

In applying these generalization, however, the doctor must recognize that each individual and problem may be affected by all the social factors that have been discussed, and that these vary from individual to individual. His task, therefore, is to identify, explore, and use these factors in the management of the consultation and the patient.

SUMMARY

1. Social factors may influence behaviour in the consultation because:
(a) Groups such as doctors, patients, and social classes may have different beliefs and norms of behaviour.
(b) Both the doctor and patient will behave according to the rules of their respective roles.
2. Social factors influence many illnesses and may be largely responsible for the patient's decision to seek help.
3. Social factors could also affect the outcome of a consultation in the way that successful outcomes are judged.

THE ANTHROPOLOGICAL APPROACH

Several important insights have been gained from studying man's 'illness behaviour' in a variety of different cultures. In primitive as well as so-called advanced societies there is a special niche for the sick and injured. Similarly, in both types of society, healers are to be found who are invested with a special form of authority. The tribal shaman and today's general practitioner have much in common.

Kleinman (1980) studied both traditional and 'western' healers in Taiwan. He showed that the traditional healer went through healing rituals which comprised three stages – the problem was given a name; some form of manipulation or other therapeutic ritual was performed; and then the problem was given another label, such as cured or improved. This is very similar indeed to the general practitioner's diagnosis, management, and cure.

Kleinman also showed that the traditional healers tended to deal with three types of problem – acute but self-limiting problems; chronic, non-life threatening problems; and somatic symptoms of anxiety. Every general practitioner's surgery will contain patients with these problems.

Healers have in common the authority invested in them by the society. Patterson (see Osmond 1980) has called this form of authority 'Aesculapean', and has divided it into three constituent parts:

1. *Sapiential authority*

This is the right to be heard derived from knowledge or expertise. This is only one part of the doctor's authority, however, since a biochemist may have more expertise in a particular branch of medicine, but it is to a physician to whom a patient will turn when in need.

2. *Moral authority*

This is the form of authority which derives from the doctor's Hypocratic motive to do good for the patient. In addition, societies strongly approve of doctoring, so their behaviour is seen as socially right, as well as individually good and this is a powerful combination.

3. *Charismatic authority*

This is the most difficult element to describe and stems from the original unity of medicine and religion. In our culture it has to do with the possibility of death and the magnitude of the issues with which the doctor deals. This is one reason for the doctor's priestly role and it implies a desire to see the practice of medicine as something of a mystery – a desire to supplement sapiential authority with an ineffable factor which might hold out hope against the odds.

It is not just patients who invest power in doctors, however – doctors can be motivated by the desire to wield power and authority themselves. Waitzkin and Stoeckle (1972, 1976) point out that a doctor's need to wield power may affect the way in which he consults. General practitioners can increase their power over their patients in several ways. One way is to surround themselves with the trappings of power – white coats, impressive gadgetry, large desks, attached (subservient) staff, large impersonal health centres, and so on. A much more subtle way in which the doctor can increase his power is by the restriction of information to the patient about the patient's condition and its management. This enhances the doctor's sapiential authority. Powerful rituals, such as examining and prescribing, are the more charismatic in the absence of adequate explanations.

Anthropologists have also drawn attention to the distinction between disease and illness. Diseases are named pathological entities which have been identified by doctors. In order to make the present basis of scientific medicine tenable, they are said to be universal and to have properties which are independent of the person in whom they are found. This is consistent with the desire to define health in terms of the absence of certain physical and biochemical states. Each disease is thought to have a specific aetiology and natural history.

Illness is a wider concept and is defined in terms of the patient, rather than an impersonal part of the body. It includes the response of the patient to problems, how a problem affects the patient's behaviour or relationships, the patient's past experiences of illness and the meaning he gives to the experience (see McWhinney 1981; Helman 1981).

Helman (1981) has suggested that folk models of illness are based on the patient's desire to answer six questions with reference to a particular problem:

1. What has happened?
2. Why has it happened?
3. Why to me?
4. Why now?
5. What would happen if nothing were done about it?
6. What should I do about it or whom should I consult for further help?

Most symptoms are not referred for any medical attention at all (Hannay 1979), but we shall see that when a patient does come to see a doctor he already has a theory about what has happened to him. With this theory he has attempted to answer some of these questions. The answer may be a unique blend of idio-syncratic beliefs which are shared in the culture, but the doctor's understanding of the problem must include an appreciation of the patient's own under-standing – whether or not the patient's view is 'accurate' in the opinion of the doctor.

These ideas have also been explored by sociologists and social psychologists (see pp. 5 and 14).

SUMMARY

1. Society has a special role for the sick and the healers.
2. Society invests authority in its doctors. This authority consists of three parts: sapiential, moral, and charismatic.
3. Anthropologists have helped to distinguish between disease and illness and researched folk models of illness.
4. A folk model has been described and its implications for the patients' and doctors' understanding discussed.

THE TRANSACTIONAL ANALYSIS APPROACH

This approach regards the consultation as a series of transactions between doctor and patient. At any one time either individual may be said to be exhib-iting the feelings and behaviour characteristic of one of three states of mind or 'ego states'. These are:

1. **The parent** who responds automatically without working out the likely reaction. The parent commands, directs, prohibits, controls, and nurtures. For the parent, 'many things are done because that's the way they are done' (Berne 1964).
2. **The adult** who sorts out information and works logically.

3. **The child** who produces intuition, creativity, spontaneous drive, and enjoyment.

These three ego states play an important part in everyday life. Together, they are thought to represent the personality of each of us, and with a little practice, we can learn to distinguish one state from another by the words used, the voice-tone, and body language.

According to transactional analysis, each person exhibits one of the above states in any conversation, but can shift from one state to another with varying degrees of ease. People will tend to respond appropriately to the offer or stimulus of other people. For example, an adult stimulus is likely to produce an adult response and a parental stimulus is likely to produce a child-like response.

Communication can, however, break down in some 'crossed' transactions. For example, when the doctor makes an adult offer, such as 'How would you like me to help you?' to which the patient responds in a child-like way 'I don't know doctor. I'm in your hands'. Similarly, the patient might make an adult offer by asking 'What do you think is wrong with me?' to which the doctor might respond in a parental way by saying 'Don't worry – just take the tablets'.

The value of understanding and recognizing this process is to be able to analyse the reasons why communication sometimes breaks down and to be able to use this insight constructively. If doctors wish their patients to take an adult view of their responsibilities for their own health, they must treat their patients as adults and avoid perpetuating dependency by behaving as a parent. There may, of course, be occasions when it is appropriate for the doctor to behave as a parent – for example, in the early stages of bereavement – but the doctor must recognize that he is doing this and work towards the gradual restoration of the adult–adult relationship.

The transactions between people follow each other in a predictable way and often have a predictable outcome. In simplest terms, this is described as a procedure, or ritual. When the transactions become more complex, they are described as pastimes or games (Berne 1964).

All games involve ulterior or hidden communications, are repetitive and predictable in outcome, and often end up with bad feelings. . . The game is always played for its psychological component, not for the social level meaning and therefore is not straight. Games start with an invitation or 'con' which hooks into the weakness of the other person, e.g. pride, or sentimentality, if the other person takes the hook the game is on, and will be played out to its conclusion. Games are not played with awareness (Turpin personal communication).

There is a wide variety of games, describing all aspects of interactions between people in all situations. Nearly all discussions or conversations can be seen as conforming to a game plan, including behaviour between doctor and patient in a consultation. One common example is the game called 'Why don't you? – Yes but . . .' in which the first 'player' – in this case the patient – presents a problem to which the second 'player' (the doctor) makes the suggestion which begins 'why don't you . . .'. The first player then produces a reason why the suggestion will not work, maybe by claiming that the solution has already been tried or that it is impossible 'Yes but . . .'. This game can continue until all of the suggestions are exhausted, when the first player has won by proving that his problem is insoluble and no longer his responsibility. A doctor who recognizes that this game is being played can, instead of producing successive suggestions, produce the antithesis and ask the patient for suggestions 'What are you going to do about it?'.

With an understanding of transactional analysis, a doctor may be able to recognize the roles taken and the games played by doctor and patient and may view his consultation in a new light. He may be able to look at his patients in a more dispassionate way and use that insight for the patient's benefit. The main disadvantage of this type of analysis is in its complexity and its exclusion of other factors.

SUMMARY

1. Transactional analysis describes the behaviour of people in a conversation in terms of three ego states – parent, adult, and child.

2. Communication may break down when replies do not match the initial offer made by one of those in the conversation.

3. Many transactions are predictable and may be described as games.

BALINT

The approach to the general practice consultation that has coined the eponym of Balint deserves particular mention. The work of the first 'Balint' group, described by Michael Balint in his book *The doctor, his patient and the illness* in 1957 has been a major influence on general practice over the last 20 years. Whenever general practitioners have been asked to describe their libraries or to recommend a reading list for learning, this book has always been near the top of the list.

In the 1950s general practice was at a low ebb. Thanks to the values inculcated at medical school and early hospital learning, general practice had been regarded as the sorting out of the important from the predominantly unimportant, a philosophy which led many doctors to seek their professional satisfaction in picking up 'worthwhile' cases from relatively 'unpromising material'. Balint's contribution changed the way the general practitioner looked at his work.

His philosophy has three main themes:

1. Psychological problems are often manifested physically and even physical disease has its own psychological consequences which need particular attention.

2. Doctors have feelings and those feelings have a function in the consultation.

3. There needs to be specific training to produce 'limited but considerable change in the doctor's personality so that he could become more sensitive to what is going on . . . in the patient's mind when the doctor and patient are together' (Balint 1957).

We would like to amplify the first two themes here and discuss the third in the next chapter.

The idea of psychosomatic disease was not new, but Balint gave it greater meaning for general practice. He showed that doctors are able to treat bodies and minds simultaneously. It was shown to be important, not just to diagnose psychological disorders by exclusion, but to elicit and evaluate any possible psychological factors associated with the presenting illness, in just the same way as a doctor needs to learn how to evaluate the large amount of data from modern diagnostic investigations.

For doctors to think that their feelings, thoughts, and prejudices were to be taken into consideration in the consultation was a concept in 1957 that was new and slightly revolutionary, but it was well known and established in psychology that it is impossible to look at a relationship whilst taking into consideration just one of the persons. Before Balint, people had looked at the psychodynamics of the patient and the effect of the doctor, but he found that it was only possible to understand the interaction fully if the relationship between the doctor and the patient was studied. The term 'drug doctor' was coined and Balint's initial work was to study the pharmacology of the drug, its side-effects, the fact that it is far from standardized, and patients can benefit from all varieties of it, but this did not mean that all varieties were equally beneficial.

The Balint approach established that doctors are active rather than passive participants in the consultation and showed how the doctor's feelings need to be identified and used within the consultation. Subsequent work described the flash technique (Balint and Norell 1973) where doctors become aware of their feelings in the consultation and on occasions interpret those feelings back in a way that can give the patient some insight into the problems that are presented. For example, if a patient angers the doctor it may be that other people will also be made angry and it might be appropriate to ask the patient about this.

The recent critics of the Balint approach to the patient are mainly aimed at the over-enthusiastic acceptance of the approach to the exclusion of any other. The verb 'to Balint' has been coined (Zigmond 1978), which describes a doctor's compulsive habit of offering interpretations to patients who have not asked for them. There are a number of criticisms in the same vein, but it must be pointed out that Michael Balint emphasized that his approach was to supplement traditional methods, not to replace them.

The strength of this approach to the consultation is the recognition and acceptance of feelings, both of the patient and the doctor. This has developed over subsequent years in many different ways, but the main bequest that the approach has given to the general practitioner is a role with all patients who come to him, whether they have a recognizable pathological disease or not. Not only has the role been defined, but general practitioners have been given an easily usable psychotherapeutic approach to managing their most difficult patients.

SUMMARY

1. Nearly all problems presented to the doctor have a psychological element to them and this needs exploring.

2. The doctor has feelings in a consultation. These need to be recognized and can be used to the benefit of the patient.

3. The general practitioner has a positive therapeutic role in all consultations, not only in those with a defined disease process.

THE SOCIAL-PSYCHOLOGICAL APPROACH

The consultation and its processes have been researched extensively by social psychologists. Their interest in human behaviour has led them to describe attributes of doctor and patient, such as their personality and behaviour in the consultation, but many studies have made little or no attempt to relate these to outcomes. In this section we shall emphasize those studies which have helped us to understand better how outcomes are achieved.

The doctor's personality

By personality we mean those more enduring aspects of a person which motivate or characterize his behaviour. Personality is thought to be slow to change, and if a doctor's effectiveness depends largely on his personality, selection of doctors would be far more important than training in consultation skills. In contrast, behaviour changes from moment to moment, and if effectiveness depends on behaviour in the consultation, training in consultation skills is feasible.

It is a commonly held belief that a good consultation depends on the compatibility of the doctor's and the patient's personality, and although this has not been investigated, one aspect of the doctor's personality has been shown to be related to getting the diagnosis right. Marks, Goldberg, and Hillier (1979) showed that doctors who were conservative were less able to diagnose psychiatric problems, but they also tended to ask fewer questions about psychiatric conditions. Similarly, doctors who were more empathic tended to be more able to diagnose psychiatric problems. Thus the doctor who wants to be able to improve his ability to diagnose psychiatric conditions does not have to change his personality, but, it would seem, merely ask more psychiatric questions and learn to show more empathy.

The patient's personality

Most descriptions of patient's personality, such as introversion or extroversion, tend to be unrelated to outcomes. There is a notable exception to this, however:

some people explain what happens to them largely in terms of their own actions, whereas others explain what happens to them as if they had little control over it at all. The former are said to have an 'internal locus of control', and the latter an 'external locus of control' (Rotter 1966). This distinction also applies to the ways in which people regard their health and a scale has been devised which measures whether people see their health as within or beyond their own control (Wallston, Wallston, and de Vellis 1978).

The relevance of this work for the doctor comes from a series of studies which shows that 'internal controllers' are more likely to look after themselves than are 'external controllers'. It has been found that internal controllers are more likely to ask the doctor for information, take their medication appropriately, keep to a diet and successfully give up smoking. They are also more likely to keep medical appointments (Wallston and Wallston 1978).

Some psychologists would argue that locus of control is not, strictly speaking, a personality dimension, since it can be readily influenced, but this makes the matter more relevant for the doctor – if he can help his patients to see that their health can be influenced by their own actions he will subsequently influence their behaviour. In this way the doctor increases the chances that his patients will comply with instructions given and take preventive action.

The other important attributes of the patient which have been shown to influence compliance and prevention are the patient's beliefs about health.

The patient's beliefs

By far the most extensively validated description of patients' beliefs about health and related matters is the Health Belief Model (Rosenstock 1966; Becker and Maiman 1975). This model describes five elements of the patient's health beliefs:

1. People vary in their overall interest in health, and their motivation to look after it. This element has been called 'health motivation'.

2. With reference to any specific problem, patients vary in how likely they think they are to contract it. This element has been called 'perceived vulnerability', but with patients who already have a problem, this factor may be seen as 'belief in the diagnosis', which may be affected by several factors. The patient may, for example, hold a prior-existing but erroneous health belief, and if the doctor does not discover this belief the patient may be influenced by it after the consultation is over. For example, a patient may believe that headaches are caused by sitting in a draught, and after the consultation is over, may still feel that this is a better explanation of the headache than the tension suggested by the doctor. If the doctor does not discover and deal with the prior-existing belief, the effectiveness of the consultation may be reduced.

3. Patients vary in how dire they believe the consequences of contracting a particular illness would be, or of leaving it untreated. The term 'perceived seriousness' describes this belief.

4. Patients weigh up the advantages and disadvantages of taking any particular

course of action; they do not necessarily take all the relevant considerations into account, but they do make an evaluation. This element has been labelled 'perceived costs and benefits'. Costs taken into account may not just be financial: they may be physical, such as suffering pain, they may be psychological, such as experiencing fear, or they may be social, such as enduring stigma. Benefits may also be financial, physical, psychological, or social.

5. These beliefs do not exist ready-formed for all possible problems – they are prompted or aroused by a variety of so-called 'cues to action', such as a physical sensation, a television programme, a magazine article, or a visit to the doctor.

This approach to patients' beliefs produces the best estimates of patients' compliance, of their likely preventive activity and also of their use of medical services. Jennifer King (1982) has also demonstrated that the health beliefs themselves may be determined by the patients' explanations of the causes of health and illness. Thus patients are generally engaged in a struggle to understand what is happening to them, and it follows that any doctor who remains ignorant of his patients' beliefs, or who fails to influence them, does so at great expense, since that doctor is not making use of the patients' most valuable health resource. Any doctor who wants to influence his patients to look after their health, to comply with advice and to use medical services appropriately needs to influence his patients' health beliefs.

Influencing health beliefs

The advantages of the approaches we have considered to the doctor's and the patient's personalities, and to the patient's beliefs, is that they consist of factors which can be modified in the consultation. Health beliefs, and patients' explanations of what happens to them, can be changed, so these approaches are useful and optimistic. We may therefore conclude that doctors should be actively involved with their patients' beliefs and explanations about what determines their health, since these matters influence their patients' behaviour.

First, the doctor's and the patient's expectations of the consultation may also be different. The patient who attends the doctor with a sore throat may expect the doctor to examine the throat but may find that the doctor spends longer looking in his ears, and this may be so unexpected by the patient that he withholds diagnostic information, since he does not think it is any longer compatible with the doctor's behaviour. Secondly, there is the effect of receiving sudden bad health news. A patient may go to see the doctor feeling perfectly well in response to a letter asking for attendance for hypertensive screening. This person is suddenly told that he has a problem which will be with him for life and must affect his lifestyle. It is possible that the diagnosis may be ignored or denied. Thirdly, two doctors may disagree, and the patient may prefer to believe the doctor whose news has been less disturbing.

In this sense patients are entirely rational. They act in accordance with their beliefs. Occasionally their ideas may not fit the known medical facts, and sometimes they may indicate a flight from facing a disturbing realtity, but it would be a gross error to believe that patients are not rational. Marshall Becker (1982) has described the ways in which experience of medical care and of illness conspire to reinforce non-compliance on the part of the rational patient.

A patient may get well or may not get well. Similarly, a patient may or may not comply with recommended management. These factors work together and may be represented as shown in Table 1.3:

Table 1.3.

	Patient gets well	Patient does *not* get well
Patient complies	A	B
Patient does *not* comply	C	D

Patient A has been reinforced in his compliance and patient D has been 'punished' for not following the management recommended. But in the case of patient B, any one of a number of calamities may have occurred:

• an incorrect diagnosis may have been made;

• incorrect management may have been planned;

• efficacious medicines may have been prescribed, but not in appropriate quantities;

• the patient may have misunderstood the instructions given but has genuinely tried to follow the instructions.

It is easy to see that B's efforts to follow the doctor's instructions will not be rewarded. Similarly, patient C, who gets well and yet does not follow the management planned will be rewarded for failing to comply. Spontaneous remission of symptoms brings relief to the patient, but gets in the way of the doctor's attempts to persuade the patient to adhere to advice given – unless the doctor explains appropriately.

In these ways we can see how a patient's experience of illness and medical care may conspire to reward the patient for non-compliance or to punish compliance. This is another instance of how patients may be entirely rational and yet not follow a doctor's instructions. And this is another good reason for making use of the patient's beliefs about the problem, the diagnosis and the planned management.

Behaviour in the consultation

Many aspects of behaviour in the consultation have been studied, but not all descriptions of doctors' and patients' behaviour have related it to any particular attribute of either doctor or patient. The verbal and non-verbal behaviour of doctor and patient, and the clinical content of the dialogue have all come under investigation.

Verbal behaviour

This was studied extensively by Byrne and Long (1976), who demonstrated clearly that there were consistencies in the behaviour of doctors which might be seen to constitute their characteristic style of dealing with patients.

The styles they identified ranged from doctor-centred (based only on the doctor's knowledge) to patient-centred (incorporating the patient's experience), with respect both to defining the problem and planning management. What is more, the doctors tended to maintain their styles, despite considerable differences in the problems presented by the patients, and in the patients' behaviour. Flexibility, it seemed, was rarely evident. They analysed some 2500 consultations on audio tape, from 71 general practitioners, and in so doing described the normal six phases of the consultation thus:

1. The doctor establishes a relationship with the patient.
2. The doctor attempts to discover, or actually discovers, the reasons for the patient's attendance.
3. The doctor conducts a verbal or physical examination, or both.
4. The doctor, or the doctor and the patient, or the patient (in that order of probability) consider the condition.
5. The doctor, and occasionally the patient, details treatment, or further investigation.
6. The consultation is terminated, usually by the doctor.

This description emphasizes that the doctor is usually the dominant party in the consultation, but it should be noted that these six phases were not always present, and that they were not always in this order. Some consultations omitted phases, some repeated phases, and some returned to earlier ones. What is important to bear in mind, however, is that 5 per cent of all consultations which appeared not to achieve any discernible objective, whether for the doctor or patient, were characterized by a reduced second phase – that is, a failure to discover accurately the reasons for the patient's attendance. Patients were rarely given the opportunity of considering their condition with the doctor. One other detailed finding to come out of Byrne and Long's work was that doctors whose style was typically patient-centred rejected their patients less.

Norma Raynes (1980) has also presented evidence that doctors may be less flexible than they would like to believe. She considered a series of investigative and management procedures doctors use in consultations, and found that even when dealing with vastly different presented problems, most of these investigative techniques varied little. They seemed more to reflect consistencies in the doctor's style than differences between patients and their presented problems.

As far as verbal behaviour in relation to the patient's social class is concerned, it seems that lower social class patients get a raw deal. In an interesting series of articles John Bain (1976, 1977) found that there were major differences in the extent to which he and a group of other doctors talked to patients from different social classes. This would not matter so much if the differences were only in the amount of social chat that went on, but Pendleton and Bochner (1980) have demonstrated that doctors offer fewer relevant explanations to social class IV and V patients – or rather, to patients the doctor believe to be from these classes. Coope and Metcalfe (1979) had also already shown that these are the very patients who know least about their health, but patients from all social groups express clear desires to be well-informed (Cartwright and Anderson 1981).

Finally on the subject of verbal behaviour, there has been a series of studies of the factors in the consultation which determine patients' satisfaction with those consultations. It would be out of place to review all the relevant literature here; suffice it to say that patients are more satisfied when the doctor discovers and deals with the patients' concerns and expectations; communicates warmth, interest, and concern about the patient; volunteers a lot of information; and explains matters to the patient in terms that are understood (Pendleton 1983). This may not sound too difficult, but Tuckett (1982), for example, has drawn our attention to the low level of adequate understanding in patients after their consultations. This appears to be related to poor explanations given by the doctor; in Tuckett's careful study it was found that general practitioners rarely discovered patients' beliefs about their problems, and it was rarer still that they adressed their own explanations to the patients' beliefs.

Non-verbal behaviour

Many messages are transmitted between doctor and patient without words – messages concerning emotions are most frequently expressed non-verbally, especially through facial expression, direction of gaze, and tone of voice. Doctors use these and many other non-verbal cues to form impressions of what is happening to the patient, or how the patient feels. When patients describe their symptoms, their gestures may be more accurate than the words they use, since patients are often remarkably ignorant about the location and size of bodily organs, and for this reason the words they use cannot automatically be believed. Similarly, the quality of an experience is transmitted non-verbally; we form clearer impressions of how severe a pain was, for example, by observing the way that pain is described, rather than by listening to the words used.

Patients also interpret the doctor's non-verbal behaviour. When the doctor tells the patient that all is well, the patient may well notice inconsistencies in the doctor's non-verbal behaviour which might imply a nagging doubt in the doctor's mind about the matter. Similarly, the communication of interest in the patient by the doctor will frequently be achieved by the patient noticing indicators in the doctor's posture, direction of gaze, and facial expression of responsiveness and understanding. One major difficulty, however, is that patients seem less able to judge doctors' feelings accurately in the consultation than doctors are to judge patients' feelings (Pendleton 1981), and this requires that less is left to patients to interpret, and more to be stated. Doctors in the study quoted also were not able to judge their patients' feelings with complete accuracy, however, and for this reason there is a real need to deal with matters of feelings and concern explicitly, rather than leave these matters to interpretation alone.

In conclusion, the behaviour of doctor and patient in the consultation influences strongly their impressions of what went on. The evidence points to a clear need to deal with matters explicitly rather than leave too much to be inferred.

The investigation of patient compliance

A major concern of social psychologists is how people come to influence each other's behaviour. A major concern of doctors is how to encourage patients to look after their health. These interests come together in the investigation of patient compliance with medical advice. In the last few pages, compliance has been mentioned several times, and ways of improving it have been detailed, but we have not said anything about the extent of the problem.

We are all familiar with certain paradoxical patients, such as the bronchitic patient who presents every year with a bad cough and yet who smokes heavily, and with whom advice about stopping smoking has been unsuccessful. We are also familiar with the obese arthritic patient with painful knees, who cannot lose weight successfully, despite the doctor's pleas, admonitions, warnings, threats, and so on. These rather graphic examples are symptoms of a really rather widespread problem. Literally hundreds of studies have been conducted on this subject, all types of advice have been investigated (Sackett and Haynes 1976), and many different measures of compliance have been taken, from measures of the levels of substances in the patient's body to asking the patient whether or not the advice was followed (Dunbar 1979). The most recent review to be published about patient compliance summarized the evidence in Table 1.4.

Table 1.4 shows clearly two things: first, the range of non-compliance is broad. Some advice given by doctors to some patients some of the time is followed closely, but there is the other side of the picture to consider. Secondly, the mean is fairly consistent – about half of all medical advice given tends not to be followed.

Richard Podell has presented the evidence in a slightly different way, and he talks of the 'rule of one-third'. Podell (1975) argues that approximately one-third of patients will follow advice closely enough to make it effective. A second one-third will follow some of the advice but not closely enough to make it effective, and this group will also be influenced by advice given by other people which may conflict with the doctor's suggestions. The final one-third does not accept or follow the advice at all.

Some might argue that it is not the doctor's job to attempt to influence the patient – it is the doctor's job simply to state what the patient would find helpful and then leave the matter of compliance entirely in the patient's hands. The authors do not take this view; indeed, we find it paradoxical that when patients

Table 1.4. *The frequency (%) with which patients fail to follow advice about medication (Ley 1983)*

Type of medication	Barofsky (1980)	Ley (1977)	Food and Drug Administration (1979)
Antibiotics	39	42	43
Psychiatric	39	42	42
Anti-hypertensive	–	43	61
Anti-tuberculosis	39	42	43
Other medication	48	54	46
Range of percentages not complying	8–92	11–95	6–83

seek help with a problem, and when sound advice is given in good faith, two-thirds of the advice is not followed. Certainly this needs to be explained, but frequently doctors' explanations are little more than rationalizations for their inability to influence their patients. Even if the doctor's understanding of his patients' difficulties is accurate, this is where the doctor must start to influence the patient. Whatever is hindering the patient from following the advice is part of the problem which is affecting the patient's health, and should be dealt with in the consulatation.

We have shown that the literature on compliance demonstrates that patients comply better when they believe they can have some control over their health and when the advice given is consistent with their health beliefs (Becker 1979), and it has also been demonstrated that patients who are more satisfied with a consultation are more likely to follow advice given (Korsch, Freeman, and Negrete 1971).

One major barrier, however, to patients' following advice given is, of course, if they cannot remember it, and Ley (1974) presented data from six studies which seemed to suggest that patients forget half of what the doctor tells them. More recently, however, Pendleton (1981) has demonstrated that patients remember the vast majority of the *important* information they are told; indeed, it seems that the earlier finding that patients forget half of what they are told may have been an artefact of the procedures used to calculate the proportions remembered and forgotten. Suffice it to say here that patients remember well the information their doctors want them to know, and it becomes particularly important, therefore, to ensure that patients understand the information they remember. Unfortunately, as we have already mentioned, David Tuckett's recent work has shown that patients' understanding of medical information is disturbingly low.

These findings may be reviewed along with many others in the original papers, but this briefest of summaries make it clear that the consultation is central, and that it needs to have a positive educational emphasis in order to be effective – that is, in order to influence the patient's health beliefs, and to develop the patient's understanding of the influences on his health.

There is certainly evidence that patients comply better with the advice when they have been involved in making the decision (Fink 1976). Shared decision making allows both doctor and patient to influence one another, and commitment to jointly derived decisions is usually greatest. Patients who are involved in decision making will follow advice better than those who are excluded from the decision-making process, and what is more, there may be no better way of demonstrating patients' control over their own health than for the doctor to take their point of view seriously, and to share the decision making process with them.

Attempts made by patients to influence doctors in consultations have rarely been documented. Many anecdotes may have been told of this experience by the doctors who were involved, but few systematic studies have been conducted. One such investigation demonstrated that communication difficulties were frequently experienced by general practitioners when patients made attempts to influence them (Pendleton, Brouwer, and Jaspars 1983) but it has often been stated that patients, by and large, like their doctors to be friendly, and this may also be a veiled reference to a desire on the patient's part to be involved in decision making in the consultation. This argument stems from an assumption we would tend to make about the nature of friendliness: it is rare that friendly relationships exist between unequal partners.

SUMMARY

The social-psychological approach enables us to see that it is possible for the doctor to develop the patient's understanding of his health in the consultation, and that in so doing he will influence the patient's health behaviour. In order to do this he should:

1. Discover the patient's beliefs, concerns, and expecations about the problem or problems presented.

2. Share his own understanding of the problems with the patient in terms that are readily understood.

3. Share the decision making with the patient.

4. Encourage the patient to take appropriate responsibility for his own health.

All this can only be done after the doctor has adequately defined the reasons for the patient's attendance at the surgery, but it is clear that if the consultation is to be effective, the doctor must make sure that these jobs are done.

2 Previous approaches to teaching on the consultation

INTRODUCTION

The general approaches to the consultation described in Chapter 1 have been used in teaching about the consultation. In this chapter we shall deal with four quite different teaching methods.

Both the medical approach to the consultation and Balint's approach have given rise to their own peculiar styles of teaching. Social psychology has developed a well-defined method of social-skills training which has later been developed by other behavioural science disciplines, notably sociology and anthropology. We shall deal with these under two headings – 'Teaching social skills' and 'Developments of the skills approach'. The transactional approach has given rise to a series of insights about the consultation and a psychotherapeutic technique for dealing with certain problems. There is not, however, a fully developed method of teaching about the consultation which derives from the transactional approach and it will not be included in this chapter.

TEACHING CLINICAL METHOD

The ability to take a history from a patient has always been regarded as a fundamental skill that medical students must learn during their training. This learning is achieved by a combination of instruction, practice, and feedback.

Medical students on entering the clinical phase of their studies will be given a standard framework for a medical history which will include the patient's presenting complaint and its history with each symptom clearly defined both in character and time, a general functional enquiry into symptoms that could be related to other symptoms not involved in the principal complaint, a past medical history, a family history of diseases, and a social history including factors that may have contributed to the presenting complaint or its management.

Medical students will also receive some instruction in methods of obtaining this data systematically. E. N. Chamberlain's book *Symptoms and signs in clinical medicine* describes this succinctly: 'For investigation of a medical case, a student must develop a definite system of interrogation and examination which must be carried out in a routine fashion to save time and to ensure that no important data are omitted'. During their clinical training, medical students will have the opportunity of seeing patients and developing this definite system.

Their success is monitored during the process of case presentation during which the student will be expected to present a succinct and accurate account of his clinical findings and his interpretation of them.

Students steadily improve in their ability to elicit and report clinical data accurately as they proceed through medical school. This approach has a number of fairly serious limitations, however. The standard framework for a medical history does not include the patients' own particular concerns and expectations. The very term 'taking' a history implies one-way traffic and ignores the importance of giving information and an explanation to patients and the use of the interview therapeutically. What is more, it has been demonstrated that medical students in their first year of medical education may be more skilled at dealing with people than those in their final year – they avoid emotionally difficult subjects less often and enquire more about the patients' own views of their problem. Thus, as they progress through medical school, their level of interpersonal skills actually declines (Helfer 1970).

The deficiencies of the case presentation as a method of clinical teaching have been discussed by Engel (1971). Not only does it not allow any direct observation of the students' interviewing technique, it also encourages a tendency to deal with abstractions rather than with patients.

There are other, less well-defined methods whereby medical students acquire styles of consulting, one being modelling on the example of more senior colleagues and teachers. Harris (unpublished) has identified two modelling processes, one based on preferred models in which students simply attempt to replicate the behaviour patterns of preferred teachers and another more interesting one in which students consciously reject the consulting styles of teachers they do not like.

The second method is learning from experience or feedback. We have already discussed the way that the need to collect doctor-centred information in the medical history can lead to a doctor-centred style of consulting. What is far less understood is the way that feedback from patients influences consulting styles. Byrne and Long (1976) demonstrated a remarkable stability of doctor style in the face of a wide variation of patients and problems. It is likely that doctor-centred styles which do not encourage feedback from patients tend to be self perpetuating.

SUMMARY

The limitations of the medical approach to learning consultation skills emphasize:

1. The importance of defining the purposes of the consultation because of the way that this determines the skills that will be employed.

2. The crucial importance of feedback in the process of learning consultation skills.

TEACHING PSYCHOTHERAPY AND COUNSELLING

This approach to teaching general practitioners is usually based on the work of Balint. Training in psychotherapy, it must be remembered, is directed towards the acquisition of personal skills rather than the learning of theoretical principles. Accordingly, much of the learning consists of being given feedback about the problems encountered in a particular setting and the ways of overcoming them. Acquiring knowledge about the problems and methods may be helpful but cannot substitute for direct experience. What is more it was Balint's view that the learning of psychotherapeutic skills inevitably entails a limited, though important, change in the therapist's personality.

Until 1957 the only systematic course of training for psychotherapy came from the psychoanalytic school. This required personal analysis, theoretical work, and practice under supervision. These parts were generally kept quite separate and might even be taught by different people. The change over the last 20 years has been towards an in-service training for counselling and any theoretical input has been supplied at the same time. This makes the learning of psychotherapeutic skills much more convenient for the general practitioner with a normal service commitment to maintain.

The doctor in training describes a case history and at least one consultation with the patient in question to a variety of people. Occasionally, the only person to whom the case is described is an individual tutor. In the case of Balint training, the presentations are made to a group of other general practitioners led sometimes by a psychoanalyst and sometimes by a trained GP leader. The presentation is discussed with the doctor either by the individual tutor or by the group. Different aspects of the case are discussed. In the more psychoanalytic training, the feelings and internal conflicts of the doctor are the focus of the discussion. In some training it is the patients' problems and the ways in which they might be managed which are emphasized. Balint seminars are neither primarily concerned with the psychopathology and psychodynamics of the patient (although this is needed to understand the patient properly), nor with the private conflicts and more public relationships of the doctor. It is the relationship between the doctor and the patient under discussion which is emphasized and the ways in which the relationship might be utilized more effectively in the doctor's medical work.

In this form of training, the tutor or group only find out about the patient through the doctor. This is both the strength and weakness of the approach. The presentation depends on the accuracy of the doctor's memory but in presenting his case, the doctor reveals a lot about himself and his feelings. But much may be lost because of the doctor's conscious or unconscious exclusion of some aspects of the consultation and the relationship.

Another major weakness of the method is that the time taken to achieve the appropriate level of skills is considerable. A full Balint training takes at least two years of weekly seminars – each of which will last between one and a half and two hours. Other forms of psychotherapy training require a similar time commitment.

SUMMARY

We may learn a number of important lessons from this psychotherapeutic approach to teaching about the consultation:

1. The psychological component of the consultation is fundamental and requires that we consider the doctor's and the patient's feelings.

2. Learning skills may involve changes in attitudes as well.

3. Learning in groups about these matters may be more effective than learning alone.

TEACHING SOCIAL SKILLS

This approach to teaching is well founded in social psychology theory (Argyle and Kendon 1967) and has led to a practical method of helping people to become more effective in their relations with others. This method has been called social skills training (Argyle 1969; Argyle, Furnham, and Graham 1981). Its central theme is that effectiveness in dealing with people depends on the use of a repertoire of behaviours which are learned. These behaviours may be identified and may even be taught to those who are not so effective. These people are variously called unskilled or are referred to as having social skills deficits.

Most people are effective some of the time and so attention is usually directed towards specific deficits in particular settings. A doctor, for example, may be able to take a history from most patients but may find adolescent girls especially difficult to deal with. The doctor may learn how to deal with this group of patients from someone who gets on well with them but who may find elderly men rather difficult. Thus each doctor may have skills in some areas but deficiencies in others.

Social skills training, as it is typically carried out, comprises three distinct phases. First, goals have to be specified. A goal which a general practitioner might want to achieve would be to have his obese patients lose weight. Secondly, a comparison is made between the behaviour of those individuals who are able to achieve the goal and those who are not. In our case, this would mean a comparison of those general practitioners whose patients lose weight successfully with those whose patients do not lose weight. Thirdly, novices, or those who are not usually effective, are taught to do what is effective and the change is measured.

All of this is simple, clear, and entirely logical but frequently the second phase is omitted since it is time consuming. When this happens, goals are specified and then an 'expert' assumes that he knows what usually leads to success. Teaching thus becomes based on the assumptions of the expert.

The social skills approach has been used successfully in a wide range of contexts. Mental patients, criminals, salesmen, and professional groups have all benefitted from social skills training (Argyle *et al.* 1981). The medical profession will normally encounter social skills training in the form of training in interview skills in medical school. In the United States, most schools came to use this technique during the 1970s. Carroll and Munroe (1979) described the rapid growth of skills training and have also cited a considerable amount of evidence that the technique is generally effective, that is, that the behaviour of the students changes significantly and in the prescribed direction.

In the United Kingdom, several schools have introduced skills training but the development has been much slower (Wakeford 1983). This teaching has normally been didactic – that is, an experienced clinician has specified how an interview should be carried out and this has been taught. Teaching of this kind is a relatively straightforward matter. First, the 'good' interview is described (for example on a handout) and might even be demonstrated by an expert. Secondly, each medical student is asked to perform an interview in the same way and usually this is recorded in some way. Audio recordings, video recordings, or verbal descriptions by another person have all been used. Thirdly, the recording is used to provide the student with feedback and recommendations are made as to how the learner might improve. This process may be repeated as many times as the teacher wishes until the student is able to perform satisfactorily.

This form of teaching has become very sophisticated. Possibly the best example is to be found in the work of Maguire, Roe, Goldberg, Jones, Hyde, and O'Dowd (1978). Forty-eight medical students were trained using one of four different methods. One group (the control group) received the usual training in history taking provided by their clinical firm. The remaining 36 students received one of three types of feedback training. This training was provided by tutors who used video-tape replays, audio-tape replays, or ratings of practice interviews conducted by the students. The control group showed little improvement. By contrast, all three feedback groups improved their ability to elicit information which was considered to be relevant. Only the audio and video groups also showed improvement in the behavioural techniques which were thought to be desirable. Although there was no significant difference between these two groups, the students preferred the television group.

The social skills approach is highly successful in teaching well-defined skills but in general practice there are fundamental difficulties in using it. Whilst it is helpful to regard the ability to deal with patients as skilful, there is no clear agreement on the goals of the general practice consultation. Any attempt, therefore, to teach skills tends to become based on the preferred consultation style of the teacher. But without any clear statement of what the consultation is to achieve it is impossible to justify dogma concerning style. General practitioners with vastly different styles might prove to be equally effective. This would call into question insistence on either style. One general practitioner may concentrate on open questions (such as 'How did you feel at the time?') whereas another general practitioner may only ask closed questions ('Did you feel any pain?') but each may elicit equally helpful information. One doctor may sit formally facing his patient across the desk, whilst another may sit knee-to-knee with his patient with the desk out of the way. But who is to say which style is preferable? It could be argued that it is up to the patient to choose but different patients may prefer different styles.

What is needed is a clear and coherent statement of what the consultation is expected to achieve. Without this, the teaching of skills cannot be rationally based.

SUMMARY

1. Effective consulting is skilful.
2. Skills can be learned by providing feedback.
3. To use this effective approach to teaching, it is first necessary to specify what the consultation has to achieve.

DEVELOPMENTS OF THE SKILLS APPROACH

It has been a frequently made criticism that both the social skills model and the training which has derived from it ignore the feelings of those involved (Pendleton and Furnham 1980). In a number of training programmes, this aspect has been introduced, whilst maintaining many other aspects of social skills training.

'Interpersonal process recall' is an approach to training developed by Kagan, Schaube, Resnikoff, Danish, and Krathwohl (1969). The learner is recorded on video-tape conducting an interview. When the recording is subsequently reviewed by the learner and teacher together, it is the learner who selects those aspects of the interview which are to be discussed. The role of the teacher is not to teach desired behaviour but to help the student to understand what he experienced and what he did. To this end, the teacher might encourage the student to describe what happened in the interview and might then point out any notable consistencies in the description. An example might be the student who rarely mentions or notices how he was feeling during the interview. When the student notices this omission in his account and in his use of the video-recording his attention is drawn to the matter and his behaviour may be influenced. The advantages of this approach are that the learner chooses what should be discussed and that it allows feelings to be explored as well as behaviour.

Another development of the social skills approach employs actors to simulate patients. This is thought to be preferable to using patients in the training for a number of reasons. One clear advantage is that the teacher is able deliberately to prepare the actor to present those aspects of a case on which the teacher would like to dwell. What is more, the actor may be able to produce particular behaviour 'to order' and this allows the learning to be carefully planned.

Certainly those actors who are able to maintain their role, not only in the interview but also in the subsequent discussion about the interview, allow alternative suggestions to be explored. This technique requires experienced actors since staying 'in role' for long periods of time can be disturbing to them. Another helpful feature of this approach is that these vocal 'patients' can provide feedback themselves to the doctor. The departments of general practice at Cardiff and Manchester Universities have pioneered some of these techniques and in this way have been able to teach interviewing techniques to medical students most successfully.

A further adaptation of social skills training uses groups of peers alone to provide feedback to each other about their work. In a study by Verby, Holden, and Davis (1979), experienced general practitioners were recorded on video-tape whilst consulting with their patients. These general practitioners subsequently met regularly as a group to review each other's work. No model of a 'good' consultation was provided, nor were criteria suggested *a priori,* but these doctors provided feedback to each other. After a period of several months of meetings, these same general practitioners were re-recorded and the 'before' and 'after' video-tapes were randomly presented to independent judges. The judges rated how well the doctors had used a series of behavioural skills, and it was found that the doctors' use of more than half the skills had improved.

SUMMARY

Developments of the social skills approach have paid closer attention to the feelings of the doctor in training, to the potential feedback from the patient and to the feedback which can be provided by peers.

3 Around the consultation

INTRODUCTION

We suggested in Chapter 1 that, since the consultation is the central act of medicine, it deserves to be understood. We have reviewed several rather different approaches to the consultation and have seen that each has its strengths and its limitations. Each approach has much to contribute but we have argued that we need a more comprehensive and coherent understanding of the consultation than any or all of the approaches afford.

In this chapter we shall begin to construct a rationale which we believe is comprehensive and coherent. We shall place the consultation in its chronological context. The sequence of events that lead up to a consultation and those that follow it will help us to see what should be done in the consultation. In this way we shall treat the consultation as a 'black box', but in the following chapter we shall look inside it.

ANTECEDENTS OF THE CONSULTATION

We begin with an individual in a healthy state. It is not necessary here to produce an exhaustive definition of health, since health is hard to define, and it is sufficient for our purposes to adopt the World Health Organization's definition, which speaks of physical, psychological, and social well-being, not merely the absence of disease (Constitution of the WHO). This definition is very broad, and few could claim to be in such an ideal state for long periods of time. People need to understand, however, that the 'state' of health is not without its ups and downs – 'health' fluctuates, and changes in health are normal. Everyone keeps a check on his health as it changes and usually ignores the changes in his physical, psychological, and social state, regarding them as unremarkable. Some of these changes may be regarded as symptoms by a doctor, but this fact alone is neither necessary nor sufficient for anyone to consider seeking help or advice.

It is the minority of 'symptoms' experienced which are presented to a general practitioner (Hannay 1979), and, despite the commonly held belief of the medical profession, there is a tendency for people to under-use their doctors. Long before anyone makes an appointment to see a doctor he attempts to make sense of the changes in his health, and we have seen in the first chapter of this book that all of us have attitudes and beliefs about health, illness, and medical treatment which constitute our 'health understanding' (Pendleton 1983).

Health understanding may be made up of many isolated pieces of accurate information as well as misconceptions, myths, irrational beliefs and fears. Much of the research on patients' health beliefs has shown, however, that patients attempt to weigh up their chances of succumbing to a particular problem (how likely am I to get X?). They also try to work out how serious the problem would be if they were to get it (how serious would X be for me?), and next they calculate the costs and benefits which would be involved in treatment (what are the pros and cons of having X treated?). Naturally, all this has to be considered against the individual's overall concern about his health, but everyone seeks answers to these questions whenever he thinks his health is threatened. What he does about it also varies. Some people believe that their health is beyond their control – they may believe that it is in the hands of fate. Some put their confidence in other people – their bosses, their family and friends, or their doctor – and these people look to those around them to protect their health. But many regard their health as their own affair and attempt to look after themselves well.

In Chapter 1, p. 15 the considerable evidence for these claims has been presented, and we have come to see that each individual has his unique health understanding and that this governs to a large extent both his attempts to look after himself and his decisions to use health services.

Changes in health may include the effects of a problem (Tuckett 1976). A man with a frozen shoulder may be more concerned about the effects of his problem on his ability to play golf than about the broader implications for his health *per se*. Similarly, a mother who has lost her voice may find that her relationship with her family is disrupted, and it may be this effect of a cold which she wishes to discuss with the doctor, rather than the cold itself.

The person who attributes some significance to a change in his health and interprets it as a problem may then do one of three things. He may choose to do nothing, to treat it himself, or to seek help. If the choice is to seek help, it may be the help of a friend or relative, a social worker, priest, acupuncturist, faith healer, or even a doctor. The course of action chosen is influenced by the person's health understanding and will usually also be discussed with a relative or friend (Pendleton 1981).

Thus, when an appointment is made to see a general practitioner, the patient has already considered the matter and will come to the doctor with ideas, concerns, and expectations about the problem and its treatment. Consider the following example: a man of 42 experiences pains in the chest whilst playing golf. These pains are relatively minor and are dismissed as unimportant. The pains occur again whilst he is working in the garden. He thinks that it is odd that the pains have occurred and has a short rest. The pain stops. After several days, back on the golf course, the pains reappear and he starts to think something may be wrong. He knows that he has been working hard lately and that he has been feeling rather weak, and the thought occurs that he may be falling ill. Chest pains are never good news, and he mentions them to his wife, who expresses concern. He knows that something serious may be signified by pains in the chest and yet is rather afraid that a doctor may restrict his activities to an unacceptable degree. None the less, on balance he knows that he should see the doctor and makes an appointment. His father died with cancer of the oesophagus and he experienced pains in the chest.

This man has thought about his health to a considerable degree. He has first ignored the problem, then done nothing about it and subsequently talked it over with his wife. He has **ideas** about the problem which are that although the pains may be related to exertion – and may therefore be minor muscle strains – it is just possible that something more serious may be going on. His **concern** is that he may have the same problem as his father. He **expects** the family doctor to consider this possibility and that he will do so automatically since the doctor cared for his father until he died 15 years ago. This expectation is derived in part from his previous experience.

Patients come to a doctor with an understanding of their problems which may be incomplete, rudimentary, and inaccurate, or it may be elaborate and entirely in agreement with current medical opinion. But the patient has a theory and it is influencing his behaviour. The weight of evidence from studies of patients' use of medical services serves to reinforce the argument here (Kasl 1974; Zola 1972, 1973; Becker, Haefner, Kasl, Kirscht, Maiman, and Rosenstock 1977; Pennebaker and Skelton 1981; King 1982).

We may summarize the events which lead up to a consultation as in Fig. 3.1.

CONSEQUENCES OF THE CONSULTATION

All consultations have effects or 'outcomes', and some effects will be **immediate**. Patients' concerns may have been influenced – they may have been increased, decreased, or removed altogether. Patients will probably remember most of what the doctor said, but may well not understand it clearly (Pendleton 1981; Tuckett 1982), and they may be more or less satisfied. Similarly, patients may be more or less committed to carrying out the plans made in the consultation.

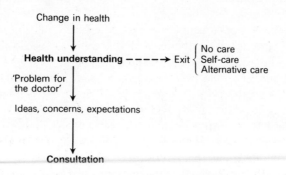

Fig. 3.1. The consultation's antecedents.

These immediate outcomes may be measured as soon as the consultation is over – they are extremely likely to have been influenced by what happened in the consultation, but may not be. If the consultation did not cover some of the patient's ideas and concerns, or if it did not deal with the patient's expectations, the effects of the consultation may be rather more limited than they need be.

If we return to our earlier example, we may see how the consultations's immediate effects might work. Our 42-year-old man with chest pains arrives at the doctor's surgery and sees his family doctor. On hearing the man's story, the doctor assumes that he is concerned about his heart. He thoroughly examines the patient, carries out an ECG, and announces with great emphasis that his heart is fine. The patient is somewhat relieved that the doctor seemed so positive, but what about his throat? The doctor did not mention this at all and he has already taken 20 minutes of the doctor's time. He decides not to mention his throat, but is not sure what to think now – did the doctor really think that something *was* wrong with his throat but did not want to tell him? Did the doctor forget to think about his throat? Did the doctor get it wrong? What is he to believe? He is left almost as unsure as he was when he made the appointment, and his concern is as high as ever. His expectations were also not met, and he did not mention them, in deference to the doctor.

Some time after the consultation its **intermediate** effects may be seen. The intermediate effect which has received most attention is compliance with the medical advice given in the consultation – compliance, we have seen, may be influenced by the consultation's immediate outcomes. There is evidence linking compliance with patient satisfaction; with patients' memory for, and understanding of, the advice given in the consultation, and with patients' intentions to follow the advice (see Chapter 1). Compliance is also influenced by the complexity of the advice given, but the most accurate predictions of patient compliance come from patients' health understanding.

This serves as a strong reminder that the patient's health understanding needs to be developed in the consultation. The doctor needs to know what sense the patient has made of what has happened to him (his ideas), and also the nature of the patient's concerns about the problem and what he expects, as this will provide the basis of the doctor's explanation to his patient. Explanations are appreciated and, if the patient's health understanding is to be developed, they are required. The object of this aspect of the consultation is to achieve a shared understanding of the problem between the doctor and his patient.

On the basis of a shared understanding of the problem the doctor and patient together can plan the management of the problem. We know that patients follow advice much more closely when they have been involved in making the decisions (Fink 1976), and we also know that patients who believe that their health is under their own control look after themselves better (Wallston *et al.* 1978). Thus the patient's involvement in the decision making is not merely a device for ensuring better compliance – it is in the patient's best interest. A more appropriate term for 'compliance' would therefore be 'adherence to a shared plan', since this does not imply authoritarian behaviour on the part of the doctor.

Our man of 42 with chest pains may have been advised to stop smoking in his consultation, so that his risk of contracting a heart condition might be decreased. What is his likelihood of following this advice? The doctor remained ignorant of his patient's ideas, concerns and expectations, and so made no *relevant* contributions to his health understanding. What is more, he had no part in the decision to stop smoking – how could he have been involved, when the doctor and patient did not share a common understanding of the problem? He understands the advice, but does not see its relevance; he believes that smoking only affects his lungs and his heart, but not his throat. And anyway, the doctor did not examine his throat, so he decides that his visit was a bit of a waste of time. The doctor was very warm and friendly and gave an unusual amount of time, but he is not committed to the management plan and will continue to smoke. His father did not smoke – and look what happened to him – so he reasons that there's no point in giving up something he enjoys.

Whether or not the patient follows the advice given will influence the consultation's **long-term** effects, such as changes in the patient's health. Efficacious medication taken properly may improve a patient's health – the patient may be cured, the symptoms may be relieved or the chronic condition may be controlled. Similarly, if the plan was to give up smoking or go on a weight-reducing diet, the potential benefits will be lost if the patient does not adequately adhere to the plan. Thus the consultation's effectiveness depends on the patient's adherence to a sound plan; the doctor's effectiveness rests on his ability to help his patients look after themselves; the patient's well-being is dependent on his health understanding, and all are inextricably linked together.

In the patient's attempt continually to make sense of changes in his health, the long-term effects of the consultation will play a part. Changes in health will almost certainly be linked to those events which preceded them. A patient with a flu-like illness may come to believe that brandy cures it if improvement follows a large tot at night, and in the same way, a patient may come to believe that antibiotics cure the condition if the doctor prescribes them with no explanation. In both cases, the patient develops a superstitious belief – in the case of brandy, the superstition may be developed to the detriment of the doctor–patient relationship, and in the case of antibiotics, the doctor is contributing to a superstition which increases the patient's dependence on the doctor. Neither is in the long-term interests of either doctor or patient. Thus the patient's health understanding may be influenced by the consultation's long-term effects – that is, by changes in the patient's health.

Our man with chest pains, still smoking and left with his concerns and ideas unexplored, might notice that the intermittent pains disappear. He cannot attribute this to anything the doctor did – in fact he ignored the doctor's advice and got better anyway. The pains may have been muscular strain, as he first thought, but when the doctor diagnoses a mild heart condition in five years' time, with what credibility will the diagnosis be seen, and to what effect will the advice to stop smoking be given? If the doctor had explored his patient's beliefs and they had arrived at a shared understanding of the problem, the consultation may have been shorter and the effect would have been much greater. The patient would have seen the problem more clearly and would have left with his confidence in the doctor unaffected, and he would also have had his beliefs given some respect. This would reinforce his struggle to find adequate explanations for changes in his health and he would be more likely to volunteer his ideas to the doctor next time.

We may represent these effects of the consultation as in Fig. 3.2.

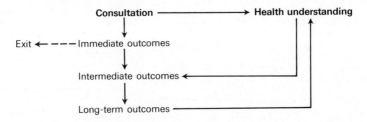

Fig. 3.2. The consultation's consequences.

THE CYCLE OF CARE

From the two diagrams we may see how the consultation's antecedents and consequences come together into a cycle of care (Pendleton 1981). The effects of a consultation may influence the next consultation by bringing about changes in the patient's health and by developing his health understanding. In general practice this is especially relevant, since patients are registered with one doctor (or practice) over several years, and it is therefore important that the potential advantages of this cycle are made to work. The cycle is represented in Fig. 3.3.

From this schema we can see the crucial role played by the patient's health understanding. It is implicated not only in adherence to the management planned in a specific consultation, but also in the patient's subsequent use of medical services. Hence there is a clear necessity for the consultation to have a strong educational emphasis in order to develop the patient's health understanding. This educational function will involve discovering the patient's ideas, concerns, and expectations, and the doctor will need to volunteer information and direct his explanations to the patient's beliefs in order to arrive at a shared understanding of the problem. The doctor and patient together will then be able to work out a plan for dealing with the problem, and the patient's responsibility for carrying out the plan can be made clear and accepted. In this way the cycle of care can be made to work positively and might be seen as a spiral staircase which gradually takes the doctor and patient in the direction of

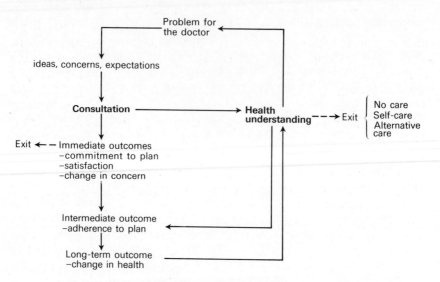

Fig. 3.3. The cycle of care.

increasingly effective health care. The alternative is the maintenance of existing health beliefs and a doctor who does not see the necessity of involving patients in management decisions, and in this case the cycle of care takes on the characteristics of a helter-skelter which quickly decreases the consultation's effectiveness.

The cycle of care has so far been described as if it were largely self-contained, but it is not. The entire cycle has to be seen in a social context – for example, any patient will probably have family, friends, and colleagues who also influence his health and his understanding of it. The effect of the social environment is ubiquitous, however, and it would be misleading to include it at any specific point in the model. The social environment influences health itself, adherence to planned management, health understanding, and the consultation. It influences the doctor and the patient. Unemployment, friends who smoke, an overcrowded home, and a wife who has no knowledge of a healthy diet might all influence the health and habits of a patient. Similarly, a doctor whose colleagues are more interested in medical politics than patient care, an unhappy marriage, and a crowded waiting room will all influence the doctor.

Clearly, the social environment will determine much of our attitudes and behaviour, but we choose and may influence our environments (Argyle *et al.* 1981). Thus a mother's health and her health beliefs may be strongly influenced by her family, but she can also influence her family's health and health beliefs. She can select their diet and may influence them strongly to give up smoking. The consultation's educational emphasis may, therefore, have an effect which is greater than was intended. The doctor who can influence a parent's health understanding may also influence the family.

Most of our attention on the cycle of care has been directed towards the patient, but the influences on the doctor could also be represented similarly. For the doctor, health understanding is usually called medical knowledge, but medical 'facts' change rapidly. What was 'known' ten years ago may well be wrong today – the field of therapeutics suggests several examples of treatment which has changed drastically and drugs which are no longer regarded as safe. Thus the doctor's 'medical knowledge' is also a form of health understanding, and the doctor's attitudes and beliefs influence the doctor's behaviour just as the patient's beliefs influence the patient's behaviour.

We have been able to cite a large number of studies which have described the patient's cycle of care, but there are very few which have investigated the doctor (see Pendleton 1983). We know that when job satisfaction is low (a long-term outcome of many consultations), the doctor is more likely to prescribe tranquilizers for his patients. This may indicate a bad effect of a poor long-term outcome on the doctor's decision making (Melville 1980). The reasons for low job satisfaction have been considered by Pendleton and Schofield (1983) – in order for job satisfaction to remain high, a doctor needs clearly defined aims and supportive feedback to tell him how he is doing and how he can improve. The general practitioner, typically, has neither. It is not surprising, therefore, that a substantial number of general practitioners regard a high proportion of their consultations as trivial (Mechanic 1970; Cartwright and Anderson 1981).

In order to have clearly defined aims, the general practitioner needs to understand the demands that are made of him. He clearly has a responsibility to diagnose and treat disease when this is present, and this is the role for which medical school has prepared him best. Unfortunately, as we have argued in Chapter 1, pp. 1–5, this model of disease and diagnosis does not fit general practice at all well, as the opportunities for diagnosing 'diseases' *per se* are few. Most patients present with problems which are best described in physical, psychological and social terms, and the idea of a clinical diagnosis is therefore too limited for general practice. Instead, the general practitioner has to define the problem(s) with which the patient has come to see him, and this will require specifying more than just the nature and history of the problems and identifying their causes. It also required that the patient's ideas, concerns, and expectations are explored, and the effects of the problems.

In terms of managing problems in general practice, the idea of treatment is also too limited. Treatment may not be necessary but all problems have to be dealt with (managed) appropriately. The terms 'diagnosis' and 'treatment' are therefore unhelpful, but the general practitioner does have roles in defining and managing the patient's problem(s), and these roles are well accepted by general practitioners.

The other role which is broadly accepted by most general practitioners is their role in 'support' or in 'caring'. Few general practitioners will disagree that part of their job entails 'caring' for patients, but exactly what is entailed in 'support' is far from clear. Support is one way of dealing with a patient's concerns; when a patient has a terminal illness, the doctor may be able to alleviate suffering and might in this way deal with a patient's fear of suffering. At other times the doctor may use his authority to reassure someone who has an irrational fear, and it is possible to regard the doctor–patient relationship as a therapeutic tool in this sense. It may be possible to deal with a patient's concerns by providing information, or to deal with the pressures on a patient by teaching the patient to relax. All these actions may be supportive or caring, inasmuch as they reduce the patient's concerns or help him to cope.

A fourth role, which is much more contentious, is the doctor's role in prevention. The medical profession recommends preventive medicine to its members (for example, The Royal College of General Practitioners 1981*a*,*b*), and prevention is said to be of three kinds. Primary prevention is the attempt to reduce the risk of contracting a disease. Secondary prevention is the early detection of a disease so that treatment can be started before irreversible damage has occurred. Tertiary prevention is the management of established disease so as to minimize disability and prevent complications from occurring.

In order to fulfil this preventive role the doctor needs to be involved in several activities. Some of these – for example, immunization, developmental assessment, and antenatal care – are frequently organized separately, but the consultation itself offers numerous opportunities for practising prevention. Ninety per cent of most doctors' patients will be expected to come to the surgery at least once every five years. At the time of the consultation the doctor may be able to check that routine preventive measures which should have taken place have in fact been carried out – for example, checking that a child's immunizations are complete. The doctor can also take this opportunity of performing simple screening tests, such as taking blood pressures, or checking that women of child-bearing age are immune to rubella. When the doctor knows that a patient has a long-term problem, such as asthma, he might ask about this in the consultation, whether or not the patient presents with the problem.

Another method of practising prevention in the consultation which has been advocated is the offering of anticipatory guidance when appropriate. This may be done when the doctor identifies factors which may put the patient at increased risk – for example, children starting to walk and becoming liable to accident, women contemplating pregnancy, or adults facing bereavement or retirement.

Some of this has been described as health education, but the majority of this chapter has been aimed at the doctor's wider educational role. The cycle of care will work best, we have argued, when the doctor makes consistent efforts to develop the patient's understanding about their own health, which is much more than education about a particular problem at a particular time. Thus the doctor's role in education should not be included under his role of prevention.

In subsequent chapters we shall show how the doctor may obtain supportive feedback about his work, but here we have begun to specify how the general practitioner's aims might be identified. In this way the cycle of care might be made to work well for the doctor as well as for the patient.

Finally, our model suggests that if we want to decide what an effective consultation must contain, we first have to specify the outcomes we want to bring about. An effective consultation, by this definition, is one which achieves desirable effects. In the preceding pages we have begun to specify what these desirable outcomes may be and those aspects of the consultation which tend to bring them about. In the next chapter we shall identify seven tasks for each consultation. When these tasks are done well, the consultation is most likely to have its desired effects.

SUMMARY

1. The consultation may be seen in its chronological context of inputs (antecedents) and outcomes (consequences or effects).

2. Inputs and outcomes form a cycle of care, and are linked by the patient's health understanding.

3. The consultation will influence the cycle of care best when it influences the patient's health understanding.

4. The doctor's roles can be identified as problem definition, management, caring/support, prevention, and education. From these, his aims may be derived.

5. His job satisfaction will be maintained at a high level when he can be shown that he is increasingly able to fulfil his aims.

6. In order to define an effective consultation, we must first specify the desired outcomes. An effective consultation is one which achieves the desired outcomes.

4 Within the consultation

INTRODUCTION

In the preceding chapters we have described the events surrounding the consultation. When we started to look into the consultation itself and began to teach about it, our emphasis was on the various skills that the doctor needed. It was not long, however, before it became very apparent that this was not a suitable starting point, since it begged the essential question: what should the doctor use his skills to achieve?

We have therefore started again by defining an effective consultation as one which brings about desired outcomes, including the successful operation of the cycle of care. In this chapter we shall describe seven tasks which, taken together, form comprehensive and coherent aims for any consultation.

THE NEED TO DEFINE TASKS

Unless we have a clear idea of the purpose of any consultation it is impossible to know which behaviours or approaches are more or less helpful. If the purpose is only to get the patient out of the surgery in the shortest possible time, writing a prescription for an antibiotic before even looking at a painful ear is effective behaviour. If the purpose is to make an accurate diagnosis, examination is essential, and if the purpose is also to educate the patient on future management, explanation would also be required.

The tasks we are about to describe can be achieved using many different approaches and skills. We are not prescribing consulting methods – we do not want all doctors to consult like automata. This is not a recipe for a restriction of individual flair. We want doctors to define what they wish to achieve in their consultations and to be able to bring this about in their own way.

THE DERIVATION OF TASKS

In the previous chapter the consultation was placed in its chronological context, with inputs from both the patient and the doctor, and outcomes for the patient which may be seen as more or less desirable by the doctor.

The case was made that the patient comes to the consultation not only with a problem that may have physical, psychological, and social dimensions, but also with his own ideas and concerns about the problem and expectations about the medical care that he is about to receive. It was also argued in the previous chapter that the doctor comes to the consultation with an idea of his own role, which not only includes defining problems, managing and caring for patients, but also his responsibility for prevention and patient education.

We have also considered the desirable outcomes of any consultation. These may be immediate, such as the patient's clear understanding and recall of the information given, a definite committment to the planned management, and, where possible, a reduction of concern. After these immediate effects the consultation may lead to the patient adhering to the planned management, and in the long-term to improvements in the patient's health, and to a development of the patient's own health understanding.

We have placed considerable emphasis on exploring the patient's own ideas, achieving a shared understanding of the nature of the patient's problem, and an agreement on shared management, principally because of the evidence reviewed earlier that this is more effective at achieving desired outcomes.

We are not suggesting that a doctor should complete all seven tasks in every consultation, and the use of the word 'appropriate' is intended to balance ideas with reality. We will, however, argue that continued omission of one or more of the suggested tasks would adversely affect the outcome of that doctor's consultations.

The first five tasks are separate statements of what the doctor needs to achieve, while the final two tasks deal with the use of time and resources, and the creation of an effective doctor–patient relationship. These tasks therefore affect all the previous five. The tasks are set out in a logical sequence, but this is not necessarily the order in which they will be tackled in each consultation.

THE FIRST TASK

To define the reason for the patient's attendance, including:
1. **The nature and history of the problems.**
2. **Their aetiology.**
3. **The patient's ideas, concerns, and expectations.**
4. **The effects of the problems.**

It would seem self-evident that the first task in any consultation is to define the reason for the patient being there. Byrne and Long (1976) found in their study of consultations that the most frequent reason for a consultation becoming 'disfunctional' was that the doctor had not discovered why the patient was there.

In Chapter 1, pp. 3–5 we discussed the nature of 'diagnosis', in the setting of general practice, and concluded that this comprised:

a statement of the nature and cause of the patient's problem sufficient to make an accurate prognosis and plan rational treatment.

We also discussed the need for this statement to include physical, psychological, and social dimensions. This holistic approach operates at a number of levels which can be defined logically, but are often more difficult to separate in practice.

The first is **the nature and history of the problem(s)** themselves. For example, a patient with the illness that we label 'depression' may be experiencing physical symptoms, disturbed thought patterns, and altered social relationships, each of which may contribute to our 'diagnosis'.

The second level at which a combination of physical, psychological and social factors interact is the **aetiology** of the problem. The evidence that the majority of episodes of depression could be accounted for by social factors was discussed in Chapter 1. Another example is ischaemic heart disease, which we now believe to be due to interaction between physical factors such as blood pressure and serum lipids, social factors such as lifestyle, and individual personality.

It was argued that, without knowledge of the aetiology or cause of the patient's problem, management can often not be rational. Defining the aetiology of the patient's problem is thus an essential part of defining the reason for the patient's attendance. This is particularly important if we are seeking to help the patient to prevent the development of the same problem in the future.

The argument so far would probably be accepted by most general practitioners. The crucial part of the argument, however, is that if we wish to establish the reason for the patient's attendance it is not only necessary to determine the nature of the problem and its cause, but also to explore what the patient thinks about his problem and about what caused it.

As we discussed in the previous chapter, a patient comes to a consultation not just with a disease or a problem, but with his own **ideas** about the nature of the problem, its causes, its importance and its possible outcomes. Patients also have more general beliefs about the importance of their health and varying degrees of motivation to look after it themselves. In Chapter 1, we reviewed the evidence that these health beliefs are a major determinant in the decision by the patient to consult the doctor in the first place, and of his likelihood to adhere to any management afterwards. Determining the patient's ideas about the problem will therefore enable the doctor to plan appropriate management with the patient, give appropriate information and explanation, and develop the patient's health understanding. The crucial role of health understanding in the cycle of care was described in the previous chapter.

Another dimension of the patient's understanding is his **concerns** about his problems. For example, with a newly diagnosed diabetic the doctor may take great care in exploring and explaining ideas about the disease and how it should be managed, but the patient's principal concern may be how it will affect his driving licence and his job. The doctor may see no problem in a maturity onset diabetic controlled by diet alone continuing to drive, but it is only if the doctor establishes that this is his patient's concern that he is likely to explain this. If the doctor regards reducing patient's concern and giving care and reassurance to his patients as important then he must make this appropriate by first establishing what his patient's concerns really are.

The third element in the patient's health understanding that is included in the reason for the patient's attendance is his **expectations** about the consultation and the help that can be offered. These expectations will come from a variety of sources, particularly the patient's previous experience of medical care, and, like the patient's ideas and concerns, may frequently be the same as the doctor's, and are therefore met without exploration and discussion. On the other hand, there are occasions when the patient expects something which is not done (for example, having his blood pressure taken or being referred to a specialist), and it is only by establishing this expectation that it can either be met or its inappropriateness explained. There are also occasions when the doctor over-estimates the expectations; Cartwright and Anderson (1981) found that only 41 per cent of patients expected a prescription before their consultation, but 65 per cent actually received one. Doctors, on the other hand, will frequently say that they prescribe because the patient expects it, and this again highlights the importance of determining what each patient actually expects from each consultation.

Finally, the patient may have attended not because of the problem itself or his ideas about it, but because of the **effects** that the problem has had – for example, on his work, his leisure, or his relationships with other people. In Chapters 1 and 3 we reviewed the evidence that a large proportion of the symptoms that patients experience are not brought to the doctor, and Tuckett's conclusion (1976) that their motives for consulting the doctor often have more to do with some change in their social circumstances than with any change in their symptoms. If these social effects are the most important reason for patients attending it may also be that they are the most important aspect of the problem that the patient would like to change. Without determining what these are, a definition of why the patient has come, and hence the management plans, may be incomplete.

Dividing the reason for the patient's attendance in this way may at first sight seem unnecessary, complex or artificial, but one example may help to reinforce our argument that each subheading is discreet and important. A 50-year-old woman presents with backache and tiredness. Further exploration of the **nature and history** of her problem reveals that she is also experiencing early waking, loss of confidence and concentration, irritability, and tearfulness.

She also tells the doctor that she has recently moved from London to a rural area; her teenage children have decided to stay in London; she has been unable to find herself another job, and she feels very isolated. These may all be part of the **aetiology** of the problem.

Her husband is a sales manager, and the **effect** of the problem is that she is finding it increasingly difficult to take part in social functions associated with her husband's work. The reason that she has come today is that her husband is becoming increasingly concerned, and she has just said that she was unable to go with him on a promotional weekend to the Channel Islands.

Her **ideas** are that her symptoms are an inevitable consequence of the change of life, and out of her control. She says that her mother was never the same again after her change. While the doctor might expect her concern to be the effect her depression is having on her relationship with her husband, she tells him that her principal **concern** is that she might need a hysterectomy, and that she would not be able to look after her elderly mother when she comes to stay as on previous occasions she has had no help.

Her **expectation** of the consultation beforehand was that it would be very short and would involve the doctor examining her internally and prescribing pain-killers.

Different doctors might choose to explore some of these avenues more fully, and to set about helping this patient, probably over a number of consultations, in a variety of ways. It is clear, however, that it is only when all these reasons for the patient's attendance have been established that the doctor can proceed to achieve fully the other tasks for the consultation.

THE SECOND TASK

To consider other problems:
   (i) continuing problems;
   (ii) at-risk factors.

The second task is to consider those problems that are present but not presented by the patient. Continuity of care in general practice gives the doctor the opportunity to build up information about his patients and families that can be used to help him understand the problems that have presented in subsequent consultations. In addition, however, there are many problems which may continue to present in patients which may not be directly related to the problem at that time. He then needs to consider whether to raise the continued problem in that consultation. For example, a young woman whose previous consultations have been concerned with difficulties with contraception may present with an ingrowing toenail. As well as dealing with the toenail, the doctor must consider whether or not to raise the previous problems, and this decision will be affected by many factors, including the previous consultations, the behaviour of the patient, and the time available. It is not necessary for the doctor to explore every problem in depth every time he and the patient meet, but he should at least consider other problems and make a conscious decision as to whether or not to explore them further at that time.

We have previously argued that one of the doctor's roles in the consultation is prevention, and Stott and Davies (1979) included opportunistic health promotion as part of the exceptional potential in each consultation. Doctors have the opportunity to perform simple screening measures, such as taking blood pressures and cervical smears and checking on immunizations, for example, for rubella and tetanus. Doctors can also help patients with continued health problems such as smoking, and can take the opportunity of offering anticipatory guidance, for example, before retirement. Again, these need not all be done at one consultation, but these factors should be considered, recorded and acted upon as seems appropriate within the framework of the extended consultation that general practice affords.

THE THIRD TASK

With the patient to choose an appropriate action for each problem.

Once the doctor has elicited the reasons for the patient's attendance and considered any continuing problems, he must make a choice of how to respond to each problem that has been identified. These choices could include doing nothing at that time, using the consultation itself to explore the patient's ideas and develop their understanding, and a wide range of therapeutic procedures from prescribing to referral. The essential points are, however, that the actions chosen should be appropriate for both the problem and the patient, and that the patient himself should be involved in making the choice. At first sight this may be seen as abdicating some of the doctor's responsibility. Many doctors have traditionally taken the responsibility for illness away from the patient, and accepted that it was their job to cure the patient. Many patients acquiesce with this view, as it is cosy and reassuring to have someone who looks after ones health. In the short term, sharing information and sharing the decision may make the doctor feel less powerful and the patient less satisfied, but ultimately better educated patients will be more able to look after their own health and be more likely to seek medical help when appropriate. A final reason for involving patients in a decision about their own management is the evidence that patients are much more likely to adhere to plans that they have been involved in choosing for themselves (Fink 1976).

THE FOURTH TASK

To achieve a shared understanding of the problems with the patient.

Earlier in Chapter 3 we described the central importance in the cycle of care of the patient's health understanding. Health understanding was defined as the patient's attitudes to and beliefs about health, illness, and medical treatment, and it was argued that this understanding could be changed, both by the consultation itself, and by the patient's interpretation of its consequences. The consultation can be used as an opportunity for the doctor to give information to the patient, and Tuckett (1982) divided the possible content of the information that can be given into:

(i) the nature and significance of the problem;

(ii) the appropriate course of action or pattern of behaviour best suited to tackle the present episode of the problem;

(iii) the appropriate course of action or pattern of behaviour suited to prevent future episodes of the problem;

(iv) possible adjustments the patient may have to make in the light of the problem or the way it is understood.

The patient may also develop a wider understanding about other health problems and the use of health services, either because more general information was shared or, more commonly, by generalizing his particular experience in one consultation.

Giving information to patients, however, is not the same as sharing understanding. Tuckett went on to explore what he meant by shared understanding, which included not only whether patients remembered what the doctor had said on a particular occasion, but also whether they understood what the decision meant, whether they understood the relevant details, why and how the doctor had reached the decision, and lastly how the information related to the patient's own pre-existing theories and ideas about the problem.

This difference is important, since it involves:

(i) eliciting the patient's own theory and ideas;

(ii) offering explanations that fit in with this framework of ideas;

(iii) establishing that the patient has understood and accepted these explanations.

Byrne and Long (1976) found that giving explanations to patients was the phase that was most frequently absent from the consultations which they recorded, and Tuckett (1982) was able to identify explanations given in response to the patient's ideas in only 1 per cent of the consultations he studied. Cartwright and Anderson (1981) reported that patients' most frequent criticism of doctors' consultations was the lack of time and information given to the patient.

This task, however, need not be extremely time-consuming, since, if the doctor tailors his explanation to his patient's own ideas and theories, time is not wasted giving information that the patient already has, or dealing with concerns that the patient does not possess.

THE FIFTH TASK

To involve the patient in the management and encourage him to accept appropriate responsibility.

At first sight this task is fairly similar to choosing an appropriate action for each problem with the patient, but this task takes this process one stage further. Not only is the patient involved in choosing the plan, he is also involved in implementing it. Naturally, the degree of involvement that is appropriate will vary; while in some instances (for example, acute appendicitis) it is appropriate for the doctor to assume full responsibility for the patient's care, in many of the problems that are faced every day in general practice – for example, upper respiratory tract infections, obese arthritics, or even patients with chronic anxiety – the value of what the patients can do for themselves far outweighs anything the doctor can do for them. This may be uncomfortable for both patient and doctor, but Illich (1977) not only argued his belief that the process of medicalization was inappropriate, he also produced the evidence to show that it was ineffective.

Encouraging patients to see themselves as responsible for their own health may, on the other hand, be more reassuring if it avoids creating a feeling of helplessness in the face of events outside their control. In Chapter 1 the evidence was cited (Wallston and Wallston 1978) that patients who regard themselves as in control of their own health are more likely to ask the doctor for information, take their medication appropriately and adopt a healthy lifestyle.

The final two tasks are quite different to the other five, inasmuch as they relate to the consultation as a whole, rather than to any specific part of it, and the touchstone of these final two tasks is in fact the achievement of the other five.

THE SIXTH TASK

To use time and resources appropriately:
   (i) in the consultation;
   (ii) in the long term.

General practitioners in the United Kingdom almost universally report that shortness of time is one of the major constraints on their work. It is therefore essential to consider the appropriate use of time in each consultation and the appropriate allocation of time between consultations in the surgery and other activities.

If we accept that the argument for each of the five tasks that have been described is valid, and if it is appropriate to attempt to achieve each task in a particular consultation, then spending the time that is required to achieve the tasks must also be appropriate.

In Chapter 3 it was argued that each consultation should be seen as part of a cycle of care, and if this cycle is to operate to greatest effect, then the way that time is used in one consultation may have a number of important effects on the use of time in subsequent consultations. If enough time is taken in one consultation to define, manage, and explain the patient's problems fully, the patient may not need to return a second time. On the other hand, very lengthy consultations may be disruptive to appointment systems, and it may be better to use time between consultations to allow the problem to evolve and perhaps to resolve itself. Between consultations both doctor and patient may also organize their thoughts, the effects of therapy may be seen, and investigations may provide additional information.

Adopting these tasks in the consultation may also change patients' expectations about the appropriate use of time in subsequent consultations. On the one hand, the doctor who is receptive to patients' ideas may help patients to express their true reasons for attending, rather than feeling that they must wrap them up in a way they think the doctor will find acceptable. In this way the whole unwrapping process can be shortened. On the other hand, patients may come to expect that more time will be available to them in each consultation. If we aim to increase patients' understanding about the nature and appropriate management of their own problems there may be less need for them to seek medical care, but if patients are more satisfied by this type of consultation then it may be that they will see greater value in consulting with other problems in the future.

Another dimension of the appropriate use of time is the relationship between the time general practitioners spend on consulting and the time spent on other activities. If consultations become more effective at achieving the tasks that are recognized as important, and if it is found that this requires longer consultations without a corresponding drop in the frequency with which each patient consults, then the way consulting time is organized may have to be re-examined.

Resources

Time is one resource available to general practitioners; others include diagnostic facilities both in the surgery and in the laboratory and X-ray departments. The skills and time of other members of the health-care team, self-help groups and other agencies are also available, and referral to hospital consultants and other colleagues are further possibilities. Again, the appropriate use of these resources can be defined in terms of what is necessary to achieve the other tasks, and again, patients have expectations about the appropriate use of these resources – for example, whether they need an X-ray, a prescription, or whether they will be referred to hospital. These expectations are in part created by their experience of previous consultations, and while it may often be inappropriate to comply with the expectation, each consultation can be an opportunity to develop the patient's understanding about the appropriate use of resources.

THE SEVENTH TASK

To establish or maintain a relationship with the patient which helps to achieve the other tasks.

The essential point of this task is that it defines a desirable doctor–patient relationship in terms of its effectiveness, rather than any preconceived idea of good, bad, or less appropriate behaviour. While earlier tasks are fairly prescriptive about what should be considered and achieved in each consultation, this task deliberately avoids making any statement about how it should be done. The same approach is adopted in the next chapter, when we consider the range of strategies and skills that the doctor may choose to employ in his consultation.

This neither diminishes the essential importance of the doctor–patient relationship, nor does it mean that all behaviours will be equally effective in achieving the tasks. The tasks require that the doctor must not only be able to take a clear 'history' from the patient, but also encourage him to communicate his ideas and fears. The relationship must also encourage the sharing of decisions, of information and of management, and must be resilient enough to allow appropriate responsibility to be given to the patient.

SUMMARY

Seven tasks to be achieved in the consultation can be derived from the previous approaches to the consultation and the place of the consultation in the cycle of care. These tasks are:

1. To define the reasons for the patient's attendance, including:
(i) the nature and history of the problems;
(ii) their aetiology;
(iii) the patient's ideas, concerns, and expectations;
(iv) the effects of the problems.
2. To consider other problems:
(i) continuing problems;
(ii) at risk factors.
3. To choose with the patient an appropriate action for each problem.
4. To achive a shared understanding of the problems with the patient.
5. To involve the patient in the management and encourage him to accept appropriate responsibility.
6. To use time and resources appropriately.
7. To establish or maintain a relationship with the patient which helps to achieve the other tasks.

5 Strategies and skills in the consultation

INTRODUCTION

In the previous chapter we have described the tasks to be achieved in a consultation. In this chapter we will consider the variety of ways in which the doctor can attempt to achieve these tasks. We shall need to distinguish between strategies (overall plans) that can be used for each task, and particular skills (behaviours) which may be used to implement a variety of strategies. For example, when the task that the doctor is seeking to achieve is to find out why the patient has come, the strategy he has chosen to employ will determine the information that he is seeking from the patient at a particular time in the consultation, while the skills involved may be open or closed questions or the use of silence.

THE NEED TO DEFINE STRATEGIES AND SKILLS

Every doctor has a different repertoire of strategies and skills that he uses in his own consultations. Byrne and Long (1976) described this wide range of doctor's styles, but also observed that an individual doctor's style was remarkably stable, both over time and between consultations with patients who have very different problems. As a learner, the doctor may need to expand his repertoire of strategies and skills to achieve the tasks with the wide range of patients and problems that are presented to him. As a teacher, the doctor needs to understand the variety of skills that can be used to achieve each task. Doctors who teach also need to be able to analyse the skills and strategies used by a doctor in a particular consultation, and to help the doctor to be aware of, and to build on, his effective skills. If necessary, they must be able to offer new skills and strategies that the learner is able to incorporate into his own style to make it more effective.

DEFINING THE NATURE OF THE PATIENT'S PROBLEM: STRATEGIES

The traditional medical model of making a diagnosis as taught to medical students is that the doctor takes a full history, conducts a full medical examination, may obtain some special investigations, and only when all these stages are complete does the doctor formulate a diagnosis. Elstein *et al.* (1978) demonstrated clearly that this bore no resemblance to the process of clinical problem solving employed by practising clinicians, either in hospital medicine or in general practice. Fig. 5.1 is a model based on this work which shows the process of problem solving or decision making which actually operates in most fields of medicine.

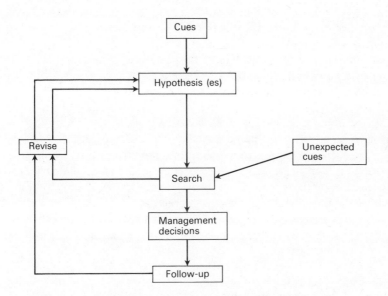

Fig. 5.1. A model of the diagnostic process (Elstein *et al.* 1978).

When the patient first presents to the doctor, the doctor receives a variety of **cues** principally from the initial offer that the patient makes, but also from the patient's non-verbal behaviour, from the context of the consultation and from the doctor's previous knowledge of the patient.

In Chapter 3 the example was given of a man aged 42 who developed pains in the chest while on a golf course. When he presents, the available cues could include the verbal description of the symptoms, gestures made to illustrate the pain, the patient's anxious demeanour, the urgency with which the consultation was requested, whether the patient had been seen for other problems recently, and the doctor's previous knowledge of the patient's family history and circumstances. Other sources of information are the feelings that the patient creates in the doctor. The use of these feelings was first described by Balint (1957), and this is discussed more fully in Chapter 1, pp. 12–14.

The next step is the formation of one or more hypotheses about the nature of the patient's problem, and it is at this stage that a number of things can go wrong. A doctor can fail to hear or observe a number of the available cues, or he may focus prematurely on one hypothesis to the exclusion of others. This may be due to the limited range of hypotheses that the doctor considers. Taking the same example, the doctor may focus prematurely on heart disease as a cause of chest pain and ignore the evidence of the patient's anxiety, or he may be unaware that anxiety can be a cause of pain in the chest of middle-aged men.

Having generated a number of initial hypotheses, the doctor can then select one hypothesis for testing. A variety of factors will influence this choice, including their relative probabilities, their risk, their potential pay-off and the doctor's degree of involvement with each type of problem. Even though the doctor may have considered that anxiety was the probable cause of our man's chest pains, he may choose to explore the possibility of ischaemic heart disease because of its risk, its treatability and perhaps his own belief about the importance of diagnosing physical illness as the prime role for the doctor.

The next stage is to test this first hypothesis by gathering further information by observation, exploration, and examination of the patient. This information may confirm or refute the initial hypothesis. A difficulty at this stage, particularly in general practice, is to obtain information which is discriminating and to decide the level of certainty that is required before proceeding, either to the management of the confirmed problem, or to test a new hypothesis. For example, the site radiation and relation to exercise of our man's chest pain may be more discriminating than the ECG, particularly if the ECG is normal. However, the level of certainty that the doctor requires may still lead him to perform the investigation.

If this first hypothesis is not confirmed, the next step is to generate and test the second hypothesis. To do this the doctor needs to use all the information which has been obtained, both from the initial cues and from the testing of the first hypothesis. In some situations it may be sufficient to establish a purely negative diagnosis – for example, that our man does not have ischaemic heart disease or any other organic pathology. The case has been made in previous chapters, however, that in the general practice consultation this still fails to provide an answer to the question 'Why did the patient come?'. There may be other reasons why our patient is experiencing chest pains, but even in their absence the doctor must still establish what the patient's own ideas about the problem are, what concerns he may have about the problem and what effects the problem may have had. The doctor needs to generate and test hypotheses for each of these questions, and it is only when they are answered that the problem can be explained and managed appropriately.

The final stage in the decision-making process is to make management decisions based on the hypothesis which has now been confirmed as a provisional diagnosis, and then to monitor the effects of the management to see whether they also confirm the diagnosis. The doctor must certainly resist the tendency to persist with a diagnosis to which he has now become committed in the face of mounting evidence that it should be reconsidered.

DEFINING THE PATIENT'S PROBLEM: SKILLS

The decision-making process that has been described is widely used, albeit with differing degrees of efficiency, and the teacher needs to be able to understand and to help the learner understand the processes involved. The skills that can be used to operate the model are, however, extremely varied, but may be equally effective at achieving each task. They have been studied extensively, particularly by social psychologists, who have also developed methods of social skills training. The limitations of this approach to teaching general practitioners was discussed in Chapter 2, but the essential point is that a variety of skills may be equally effective in achieving the same task, and it is up to the teacher to decide which skills are, or may be, most effective for each individual doctor with a particular patient and problem.

In choosing to ask a particular question the doctor must decide what information he wishes to obtain and therefore **what to ask**. He must also decide how best to encourage the patient to give him this information: viz. **how to ask**. For example, with our man with chest pain, different doctors may seek to explore the nature of the symptoms by a very open question, such as 'Tell me about your chest pain', by a more specific question, such as 'Does anything make your pain better or worse?', or by a closed question, such as 'Do you get the pain on exertion?'.

When seeking the patient's ideas or concerns the doctor might choose to ask a closed question, such as 'Are you frightened that you have heart disease?', or a more open question, 'What are you concerned that this might be?'. On the other hand, he may choose to confront the patient with a statement such as 'Many men like you are worried that they have heart disease'. The doctor may choose to use his awareness of the patient's non-verbal communication and reflect it by making a statement such as 'You look anxious about this', or he may use the feelings that the patient engenders in him and reflect them along the lines of 'You make me feel very anxious – I wonder if you are too?'.

The evidence which has been discussed in earlier chapters, however, suggests that the choice of content and type of question that is used depends more on the doctor's own style than on the particular patient and problem in each consultation. The challenge facing both learner and teacher is to learn to be able to vary and expand their repertoires according to the individual situation.

The skills of listening are less frequently discussed than those of questioning, but are equally important. It is obvious that only by listening to the answer can the doctor obtain the information that is being offered by the patient, but a large amount of information can also be obtained by observing the patient's non-verbal behaviour and in particular its congruity with the verbal messages being given by the patient. Relating subsequent questions and explanations to the information already obtained from the patient is not only more economical, but also encourages the patient to give further information. This can also be achieved by expressing interest through maintaining eye contact with the patient, by the appropriate use of silence and by the avoidance of unhelpful interruptions.

A third group of skills that must not be forgotten are those of physical examination. The prime purpose of conducting any examination in a consultation is to obtain evidence of the presence or absence of physical signs which may confirm or refute a hypothesis about the nature of the patient's problem. There are other purposes for the physical examination, however, including reassurance of the patient, meeting expectations, communicating concern, and acceptance of the patient by physical contact. It will not be appropriate in this book to describe the skills of physical examination. All examinations in every setting are selective and in the context of general practice it is particularly important to make that selection with a clear understanding of the purpose to be achieved.

CONSIDERING OTHER PROBLEMS

The major strategy involved in considering problems present but not presented by the patient in the consultation is that of record keeping. Information which is readily available in the records can be used in subsequent consultations in a variety of ways. The first is to remind the doctor of what he previously knew about the patient, and what was said and done on the last occasion that he was seen. This has obvious benefits for the doctor–patient relationship. If there are any problems which may be continuing, these can be explored and if it is clear from the records whether procedures have been performed such as taking a blood pressure, obtaining a cervical smear and carrying out immunizations, then the opportunity for health promotion can be taken without unnecessary duplication. In Chapter 3 the consultation was seen as part of a cycle of care promoting patients' health understanding. Recording the information and explanation given to patients in each consultation can also help the doctor operate the cycle successfully.

Many systems have been proposed for the keeping of medical records in general practice, but the problem-orientated system first described by Weed (1968) and adapted for general practice with the medical record envelope (Tait 1977) and with A4 folders (Zander 1978) allows the record to be used to its full potential in the consultation.

CHOOSING AN APPROPRIATE ACTION FOR EACH PROBLEM WITH THE PATIENT

Strategies for achieving this task operate at two levels. The first comprises the range of strategies which could be used to manage the patient's problems, and these may operate in a single consultation or a series of consultations. The second level comprises those strategies which can be used to **make** the choice of appropriate action for the patient and the problem.

The range of possible managements for the strictly medical dimension of patients' problems may at first sight appear clear cut. For example, for our man with chest pains the doctor might choose explanation and reassurance, he might choose to prescribe, he might choose to investigate further, or to use time as his investigation. He might also choose to refer him for specialist care.

We have argued throughout this book, however, that every patient's problem also has psychological and social dimensions, and that patients present not only with the problem but also with their ideas, concerns, and expectations. The range of possible interventions in the psychological and social dimensions is very much wider; many have been developed by highly trained professionals working from very different backgrounds. The challenge facing the general practitioner is to develop an integrated approach to the patient's psychological and social problems that can be operated in the setting of general practice.

Take our by now well-worn example of our middle-aged man. We have discovered that he experiences chest pains, is anxious, that he may have cancer, smokes, is under considerable pressure at work, only finds time to play golf very occasionally, and has an unsatisfactory relationship with his wife.

The approach that would have its roots in psychotherapy would be to develop the doctor–patient relationship, to use listening therapeutically and to explore and develop the patient's insight into the nature of these problems. The behaviourist, on the other hand, might consider one problem behaviour – for example, smoking – and explore the stimuli and gains involved in order to suggest methods of extinguishing this behaviour and reinforcing others. Behaviourists might also tackle the problem of tension by encouraging the patient to learn techniques of stress management and relaxation.

The problem-solving approach would be to explore how the patient solves his own problems and to help him develop his own problem solving abilities. The patient's problems could be broken down into manageable tasks which could be tackled in turn, the patient being encouraged by his success at the earlier tasks.

The counsellor might wish to explore the relationships within the family and the patient's own contributions to them, to explore possible means of bringing about change and encouraging the patient to choose his own strategy.

Finally, the health educator would seek to explore the patient's health beliefs, his interest in health, his perceived vulnerability to a particular problem and its seriousness, and to explore the costs and benefits of any proposed course of action.

How, then, are the general practitioner and the patient to choose what to do? The factors which can be taken into account relate to the patient, the doctor, the problem and the availability of other resources. The first factor is the patient's own understanding of his problem and his own expectations for management. To be able to make an informed decision, the patient must have a full understanding of the nature of the problem and of the proposed management. Not only must the patient be able to recall the agreed plan, he must also be able to understand it. He must know the basis on which it was reached, see how it relates to his own ideas and personal situation, and be committed to it. He must also be able to implement the plan.

The doctor's own knowledge and skills also determine the available options but a limitation on the doctor is the time he has available for each patient. A further factor is the range of other resources that are available. While it is appropriate for general practitioners to learn new skills which are applicable to their patients' problems in their own setting, doctors must also have a knowledge of and respect for the skills and professionalism of other disciplines, and be able to refer patients appropriately.

The last and most important factor is the doctor's knowledge of the nature, natural history, sequelae, and likely response to treatment of the patient's problem. Compared with our knowledge of physical diseases, our knowledge about many of the illnesses and problems that affect our patients in general practice is far more limited. The implications that this has for teaching will be considered in Chapter 7.

Many of the strategies that can help to achieve a shared decision have already been discussed. First, there is exploring and using the patient's own ideas and expectations of management. Secondly, there is choosing a management with the patient that is appropriate not only for the particular problem, but also for that patient's own situation, available support and normal coping mechanisms. Lastly, there is achieving a fully shared understanding of the nature of the problem and the proposed management, so that the patient can be in a position to make a truly 'informed choice'.

As we discussed in the previous chapter, allowing the patient to make the choice about the management, particularly of a 'medical problem', can be seen as abdicating proper responsibility as doctors, and taking a 'counselling approach' – exploring possible alternative managements and allowing the patient to choose – can be seen as only appropriate for psychological or social problems. However, it is in those very situations when doctors are most anxious that their patients should comply with the management that it is essential that their patients should understand, share and be committed to the same plan. The exercise of authority is an ironic delusion if the patient does not adhere to the management planned.

ACHIEVING A SHARED UNDERSTANDING OF THE PROBLEM WITH THE PATIENT

In the previous chapter the dimensions of 'shared understanding' were described. There are a number of strategies which can be used to ensure that this 'shared understanding' is effectively achieved. The first is to elicit and build upon the patient's own ideas and beliefs, thus offering a bespoke, rather than an off-the-peg, explanation. Not only is this more effective, it is also more economical in time and effort. The second strategy is to recognize that the whole consultation, particularly the process of eliciting, organizing, and reflecting the information the patient is giving, is an experience from which the patient can learn. Both these strategies are based on the sound educational principle that effective teaching should always be related to the learner's own needs and experience.

A further strategy is not only to elicit the patient's pre-existing ideas and offer appropriate explanation, but also to check with the patient whether all the stages of sharing understanding already described have been achieved.

Philip Ley (1976) has described a number of particular skills in presenting and organizing the information given to the patient which have been shown to increase the patient's recall of the information. He recommended that the information should be presented without the use of jargon, using short words and sentences, and as specifically as possible. For example, the statement 'You must lose weight' is less memorable than the statement 'You must lose half a stone in weight in the next month'. The order in which the information is presented also has effects; patients recall best what they are told first and items of information that are repeated. Another method is a technique called 'explicit categorization', in which the doctor first says, 'I am going to tell you what I think is wrong, what I expect to happen, and what treatment I suggest', and then expands on each of these items.

Another technique which can be effective in reinforcing the information given is the use of diagrams or leaflets that can be given to the patients. This has, for example, been shown to increase the effectiveness of the doctor's advice to give up smoking (Russell, Wilson, Taylor, and Baker 1979). It must be emphasized, however, that whether any of these specific techniques is used depends on the individual doctor, the particular patient, and the problem, but they will all operate more effectively within the overall strategies which have been described – namely, using the patient's ideas, using the patient's experience and exploring with the patient the extent to which shared understanding has been achieved.

INVOLVING THE PATIENT IN THE MANAGEMENT AND ENCOURAGING HIM TO ACCEPT APPROPRIATE RESPONSIBILITY

The degree to which the patient can be involved in his management varies, of course, with the proposed management. It can be argued that the doctor cannot invite the patient to assist in the removal of his own appendix, but there is good evidence that informing patients about and involving them in their after-care can reduce the need for analgesia and hasten their recovery. In most of the conditions and problems with which the doctor has to deal in general practice, whether managing stress or managing diabetes, the patient's contribution is vital.

To be involved, the patient needs clear information about what he should do in any given situation and what results are to be expected. He also needs to be provided with feedback about the success or otherwise of his own management. The patient needs to be able to anticipate and overcome any difficulties which he might encounter. A patient with diabetes not only needs to know the ways in which his diet should be modified, but also the goals that are to be achieved – for example, weight reduction and elimination of glycosuria – and be equipped to monitor the achievement of these goals. The patient with anxiety needs to be able to identify situations which provoke it, recognize its symptoms and learn techniques for coping with and controlling these symptoms.

Encouraging patients to monitor the success of their own management is a very powerful method of encouraging them to continue with the management and this approach is applicable to a much wider range of situations than those that have been discussed.

USING TIME AND RESOURCES APPROPRIATELY

The problem of time in the consultation and the possible effects of this approach have already been discussed in Chapter 4. A number of strategies described in this chapter can be employed to make the use of time in each consultation more efficient: determining the reason for the patient's attendance at the outset; operating the decision making model efficiently; determining the patient's own ideas before giving an appropriate explanation, and discovering the patient's own expectations before deciding on management. Specific skills can be used to negotiate a contract for the use of available time, to regulate and control the consultation, and to terminate it. Again, which, if any, of these skills is actually employed would depend on the individual doctor, the patient, and the problem.

As was discussed in Chapter 3, using each consultation as a part of a cycle of care means that many of the tasks may be achieved over a series of consultations, rather than one consultation. Adopting these strategies in the consultation may also change patients' expectations about the appropriate use of time in subsequent consultations. This has been discussed in Chapter 4 (see pp. 47–8).

A number of doctors who have adopted our tasks approach have found it necessary to extend the length of each consultation. Verby *et al.* (1979) reported similar findings. They rated consultations before and after a training programme and found that, before their training programme, there was a positive correlation in the length of the consultation and the score obtained on their rating scale. They also found that the higher scores achieved by the experimental group of doctors after training were accompanied by a significant increase in the length of the consultation.

There is also evidence that there is an inverse relationship between the length of time a doctor allows for each consultation and the average number of times a patient consults him each year. Which is the cause and which the effect is difficult to determine, but a number of our colleagues who have lengthened their consultations have also found that their consultation rate has fallen.

Whether this is due solely to the increased time available, to the way it is used, or to other factors is impossible to resolve without further evidence.

Hull (1980) and Fleming (1982) have reviewed the evidence about the way that general practitioners aportion their time. The pattern that emerges is that the average general practitioner spends just over half his working week consulting with patients in his surgery. It may be that, with improved skills of management, increased delegation, and perhaps a reconsideration of relative priorities, doctors may be able to make more time available for effective consulting.

The most expensive resources available to the general practitioner are referral, particularly to hospital services, and prescribing. There is an enormous variation in the rate at which general practitioners both refer patients to hospitals and prescribe, and the factors which lead to this variation are not fully understood. They can include the training, experience and attitudes of the doctor, the ideas and expectations of the patients, the relationship between doctor and patients, the events in the consultation and the availablity of resources. To use resources appropriately the doctor needs to be able to explore and understand these factors for each individual patient.

ESTABLISHING OR MAINTAINING A RELATIONSHIP WITH THE PATIENT WHICH HELPS TO ACHIEVE THE OTHER TASKS

The doctor–patient relationship is the subject of an extensive literature, some of which has been reviewed earlier. The conclusion is that there is no single type or style of relationship which can be identified as more effective than all others. There are, however, certain strategies and skills which can affect both communication in the consultation and subsequent outcomes.

The setting of the consultation, including such features as accessibility, waiting time, and seating position, can affect the consultation before it even begins. The initial phase of greeting patients and putting them at their ease, and demonstrating interest both in the patients as people as well as their problems, can both influence the subsequent relationship. During the consultation encouraging open communication; demonstrating to the patient the doctor's warmth, empathy, and genuineness; and offering appropriate sympathy and support have all been shown to affect the relationship in the consultation and its effectiveness in achieving satisfaction and compliance.

Achieving many of the tasks can in itself improve both the relationship and the outcome of the consultation. This is particularly true of exploring the patient's own ideas and concerns, meeting the patient's expectations, volunteering information and explanation, and involving the patient in his own management. Using time in the consultation effectively, so that the doctor can appear unhurried, also contributes to patient satisfaction.

There is a wide range of skills that can be used to promote the doctor's relationship with the patient, including questioning, making encouraging noises and gestures, demonstrating the acceptance of the patient's ideas and feelings, using body posture and touch, maintaining eye contact, ensuring that the verbal and non-verbal messages being transmitted by the doctor are compatible, and offering reward and encouragement to the patient when appropriate. Possibly the most crucial skill, for the doctor, however, is for him to be able to observe the effect of his own behaviour on the patient, and to be able to choose strategies and skills that are appropriate to the individual doctor, the patient, and the problem.

SUMMARY

1. To achieve each task in the consultation a variety of strategies and skills can be employed.

2. Strategies are the plans or choices that the doctor makes, and skills are the particular behaviours that he employs.

3. The choice of strategy or skill depends on the patient, the nature of the problem, and the repertoire of the doctor.

6 An approach to learning and teaching

INTRODUCTION

In the preceding chapters we have provided a rationale for seven consultation tasks and have suggested that an effective consultation is one which achieves these tasks. Clearly, it would have been an empty exercise to provide a definition of effective consulting if it were not possible to help general practitioners to consult in this way. In this chapter we shall describe our approach to learning and teaching – its theoretical basis and some of its techniques. In subsequent chapters we shall show how a training programme may be devised which is based on this approach.

THEORETICAL BASIS

It is not by accident that we have placed learning before teaching both in the title of this chapter and of this book. Much medical education tends to begin with a description of the facts which have to be taught and with the lecture as the most common educational method. The emphasis is, therefore, on teaching. Lecturers provide all of their students with the same information, irrespective of differences in their previous levels of knowledge. Even during the clinical years of medical education there is a tendency to want all students to see similar cases and to carry out their studies in similar ways.

We start with the learner for four reasons. First, each doctor has an unique repertoire of skills and some of these skills are better developed than others. Thus, there are doctors who can achieve some of our tasks regularly but other tasks hardly ever. Similarly, there are some doctors who can achieve all of our tasks with some patients but not with others. It would be wasteful for teachers to provide instruction to learners where it is not needed. Secondly, learners learn more efficiently when the subject matter is 'meaningful' to them. New information and new skills are learned quicker and retained for longer when they are closely related to the learner's present knowledge and skills (Maddox 1963; Child 1973). Thirdly, it is our intention to help the learner to become autonomous. This means that the learner needs to develop the ability to assess his present level of performance and to take corrective action. To acquire this ability, the learner needs to observe his own behaviour and to compare it with acceptable criteria which are well understood. Fourthly, since we are dealing with the acquisition of new skills, the teacher needs to observe the learner's behaviour and to provide feedback about what he has observed.

The intitial phase of our approach to learning and teaching involves finding out about the learner. We first need to discover whether or not the tasks we have described in Chapter 4 are acceptable to the learner. The attempt to use the tasks as a definition of an effective consultation requires that the learner is willing to accept them as such. To this end, the rationale provided in Chapter 3 has to be presented for the learner to consider. If the learner permits the tasks to be used as criteria of effectiveness, the second phase of the teaching can begin. This phase involves helping the learner to evaluate his consultations' effectiveness by rating the extent to which each task was achieved in each consultation. Frequently we have found, however, that doctors find it difficult to rate the achievement of tasks to which they have only recently been introduced. For this reason, therefore, we have found it useful first to help each doctor to recognize attempts to achieve the tasks. Consultations from other doctors may even be used at this stage and the learner is introduced to a means of describing the progress of the consultation. (This technique, which we have called **consultation mapping** is described on pp. 63–6). Subsequently, the learner is taught how to use the tasks to evaluate the consultations he has just described. For this purpose we have devised a **rating scale** based on the tasks and guidelines for the provision of feedback. (These are described below on pp. 61–71).

When the learner is able to describe a consultation, to evaluate it and to present the evaluation in a positive way, the learner is encouraged to observe his own consultations. The evaluation of consulations suggests areas in which improvement might well be achieved and these shortfalls in performances may be used as aims for subsequent teaching and learning. Suggestions may now be made which are based on the learner's existing repertoire as described by the map. The teacher may make recommendations but, for the reasons presented earlier, it is preferable for the suggestions to come from the learner. Finally, the learner undertakes to bring about these changes before the next assessment.

It is not uncommon for three arguments to be raised at this point. The first concerns the relationship between attitudes and behaviour. The approach to the consultation implied in the tasks is one which requires a considerable shift from the traditional medical model of consulting. The educational and preventive emphasis recommended may not be immediately accepted by many general practitioners. This may result in an initial rejection of our approach. But everyone tends to feel disconcerted when he feels unequal to a particular challenge and this principle may be at work here. A doctor may not feel very able at patient education or at practising prevention and this may be behind his rejection. It follows that training may not only improve skills but may, thereby, influence attitudes. Thus it is necessary merely for the learner to suspend his objections for a while in order to see that training may produce a corresponding change in attitudes. The implication for the teacher is that attitudes need not be confronted as an initial step in training but may be influenced by the development of new skills.

The second argument which arises at this stage is that training such as we are advocating will produce doctors who all consult in the same way. This real concern does not, however, persist when it is realized the extent to which suggestions made in the training are tailored to the unique repertoire of skills possessed and demonstrated by each learner.

The third argument concerns the complexity of the consultation. It is held that such a complex event cannot be captured adequately by so few categories as are provided on our consultation map. This is certainly the case, but we have found it helpful to maintain the simplicity of our map, despite its shortcomings, since it has proved to be helpful to those who want to become more familiar with the tasks.

Our approach to learning and teaching may be summarized as follows:

1. Present a rationale for the consultation tasks which is related to the learner's own experience of general practice.

2. Negotiate the acceptability of the tasks as criteria of effective consulting.

3. Teach the learner to recognize when a particular task is being attempted.

4. Teach the learner to assess the extent to which each task was achieved in a consultation and to provide constructive feedback.

5. Teach the learner to set his own aims for learning based on the evaluation of his own consultations and on clear recommendations.

6. Where necessary, allow the learner to practise the proposed changes before he attempts to consult in this way with his patients.

In Chapter 8 we shall review the various methods of direct observation (sitting-in, observing through a one-way mirror, recording on audio-tape, and recording on video-tape). Each has its advantages and disadvantages but the principle of direct observation is fundamental. In no other way can a teacher begin with the learner's strengths in consulting. In Chapter 8 we shall demonstrate the overriding advantages of using video-recordings in teaching. In this chapter we shall assume that the observation method in use is video.

A METHOD FOR DESCRIBING A CONSULTATION

Description is fundamentally different from evaluation. When we describe a consultation we merely attempt to produce a record of events which are taking place. When we evaluate the same consultation we attempt to judge how effectively important matters were dealt with.

In order to become familiar with the seven consultation tasks, we have devised the technique of **consultation mapping**. This is a technique for describing the progress of a consultation through the tasks. It is possible, naturally, to describe other matters in a consultation. For example, we may describe the non-verbal behaviour (Pietroni 1976) or the feelings in a consultation (Freeling 1983) but these descriptions, although valid, are not yet pertinent to our purposes. Subsequently we shall want to know why the consultation was as it was but, for the moment, we simply want to learn to recognize attempts to achieve each task in order that we may evaluate it.

Each time the doctor or the patient speaks, what is said may be placed under the heading of one of our tasks (unless it is totally irrelevant). Consider the following extract from a consultation:

Patient: Well doctor, I've been having trouble with my ears. They're really painful. Well, the right one's painful, the other one's OK now.

Doctor: How long has that been going on?

Patient: About a week now.

Doctor: Have you noticed anything else?

Patient: Well, I've had a bit of soreness in my throat.

Doctor: What do you think has given you the earache?

Patient: I've been swimming a lot lately and I wondered if I might have got a bit of an infection.

Doctor: Let me have a look in your ears.

In this brief extract, the patient begins by offering information about the nature and history of the problem. The doctor's first two questions and the patient's answers follow up this matter. When the doctor asks what the patient thinks may have caused the earache, he is beginning to explore the patient's ideas and when he examines the ears, he is returning to the nature and history of the problem. This extract might be plotted thus:

Here we can immediately see some of the difficulties in categorization. When the doctor asked 'What do you think has given you the earache?' was he seeking ideas from the patient or was he considering the aetiology of the problem? Clearly, this matter needs to be resolved by asking the doctor but while the consultation is in progress we need to make the best guess we can. Similarly, more than one thing may be happening at any given time. For example, as the doctor is systematically exploring the nature and history of a problem, the patient's understanding of it may be increasing. Thus, the observer may wish to make an entry in more than one category in response to just one brief portion of the consultation. If the consultation is recorded on video-tape, such matters may be resolved as and when they arise and as a teacher and a learner get to know each other such problems usually arise less often. Other problems might also need to be resolved such as whether to record questions as well as answers

CONSULTATION MAP

Each time the doctor or the patient speaks, place a mark against the appropriate heading. These marks may then be joined together so that the sequence of events in the consultation is made clear.

a. Nature and history
   of problems

b. Aetiology of
   problems

c. Patient's ideas

d. Patient's
   concerns

e. Patient's
   expectations

f. Effects of
   problems

g. Continuing
   problems

h. At risk
   factors

i. Action
   taken

j. Sharing
   understanding

k. Involving in
   management

or whether to record the intention of a question or the answer given which may not have been intended. The point is that there is not a preferable way of mapping a consultation, merely an agreed way.

In order to map a consultation, we take all of the tasks except numbers 6 and 7 (to use time and resources appropriately and to establish or maintain a helpful relationship) and set out each part separately. We exclude the sixth and seventh tasks since they cannot be seen at any particular time in the consultation. The form used for consultation is provided here.

By describing a consultation in this way we become more familiar with the tasks themselves and also with the doctor's attempts to achieve them. There is no clear relationship, however, between how often a doctor attempts to achieve a task and how well it is done. A doctor may ask ten questions about the effects of a problem but may not put any of them clearly with the result that the effects of the problem are inadequately explored. Another doctor may ask just two questions but may choose them so carefully and put them so well that the effects of the problem are explored completely. After the mapping exercise has been completed, one might legitimately want to judge how well each task was achieved. We shall deal with this next.

A METHOD FOR EVALUATING A CONSULTATION

In order to evaluate a consultation, we have devised a **consultation rating scale**. This is based on the consultation tasks in the same way as is the consultation map. Each individual part of each task is rated separately and we have chosen to set out the rating scale in the form of opposing statements linked by a line. The rater is asked to place a mark (/) on the line in such a way that it represents how much he agrees with the opposing statements. The first pair of statements is:

Nature and history of problems adequately defined	a b c	Nature and history of problems defined inadequately

If the rater thought that the nature and history of the problems had been defined adequately, he might place his mark at point a. If he thought that the nature and history had been inadequately defined, he might place his mark at c. If he thought that the nature and history of the problem had been defined in part but that more should have been established in order for the nature and history to have been adequate, he might place his mark at point b. In most general practice consultations, however, there is more than one problem presented (Tate, in preparation). In this case, instead of placing a mark on the scale, the rater might want to place a 1 when he is rating the way in which the first problem was dealt with, a 2 when rating the way in which the second problem was handled, and so on.

CONSULTATION RATING SCALE

Please evaluate the consultation you have just seen by rating it on the following scales. Place a mark in such a position along each line to show how much you agree with each statement.

1.	Nature and history of problems adequately defined	Nature and history of problems defined inadequately
2.	Aetiology of problems adequately defined	Aetiology defined inadequately
3.	Patient's ideas, explored adequately and appropriately	Ideas explored inadequately or inappropriately
4.	Patient's concerns explored adequately and appropriately	Concerns explored inadequately or inappropriately
5.	Patient's expectations explored adequately and appropriately	Expectations explored inadequately or inappropriately
6.	Effects of problems explored adequately and appropriately	Effects of problems explored inadequately or inappropriately
7.	Continuing problems considered	Continuing problems not considered
8.	At risk factors considered	At risk factors not considered
9.	Appropiate action chosen for each problem	Inappropriate action chosen
10.	Appropriate shared understanding of problems achieved	Shared understanding not achieved or inappropriate
11.	Patient involved in management adequately and appropriately	Involvement in management inadequate or inappropriate
12.	Appropriate use of time and resources in consultation	Inappropriate use of time and resources in consultation
13.	Use of time and resources in long-term management appropriate	Inappropriate use of time and resources in long-term management
14.	Helpful relationship with patient established or maintained	Unhelpful or deteriorating relationship with patient

This kind of scale has the advantage that a wide range of opinions may be expressed. Small differences may also be recorded although this is only an advantage if the judgements are reliably made. It has the disadvantage that a judge can always use the midpoint and never commit himself to a firm opinion but this disadvantage is removed when recommendations have to be made. We shall describe this more fully in the following section on feedback. The consultation rating scale is provided here.

It is important to undestand how the words 'adequately' and 'appropriately' have been used in the rating scale. Here they are more in evidence than in the original list of tasks. If we take the fourth part of the scale, which deals with the exploration of the effects of the problem(s), we may first want to judge whether the effects of the problems should have been explored at all. If the effects of a problem cause particular distress, such as the disruption of a happy home, and if these effects have recently been explored at great length, it may be inappropriate to explore them in the present consultation. In these circumstances, a skilled exploration of the effects of the problem may be marked down on the grounds of inappropriateness. More commonly, if an exploration of the effects of a problem was entirely appropriate but not carried out adequately, the rater will mark down this aspect of the consultation on the grounds of inadequacy. Thus, either an inappropriate or an inadequate exploration will be marked down.

A METHOD FOR GIVING FEEDBACK

The aim of our evaluation is to provide information to the doctor so that he may learn to become more effective. This requires that the doctor should be both willing and able to change his behaviour in the light of the feedback given. If the feedback itself makes the doctor unwilling to change or unable to change then the feedback is wasted. The following guidelines generally ensure that the feedback given is useful.

Giving feedback which merely shows how perceptive the teacher or how unskilled the learner is likely to produce resistance to change. Feedback which only emphasizes the learner's failures or omissions leads to the learner defending what he did and arguments ensue. Unfortunately, our experience has led us to believe that this negative criticism is all too frequent. It is the legacy of medical education and of academic life.

Feedback given in general terms is also common but this, too, leaves the learner unable to change. If we notice that the doctor frequently interrupts his patients, we may tell him that he is domineering or rude. But the doctor who is told not to be rude to his patients may not know what to change. Does he have to change his personality? No, he merely has to stop interrupting. Thus, the specific feedback is helpful and the general feedback is, at best, superfluous and, at worst, counter-productive.

The provision of feedback should be geared to the learner's needs – both in terms of its quantity and its quality. Even feedback which is positive and specific may be given at too great a rate or at too sophisticated a level. If a young and inexperienced general practitioner is told that he should use his feelings as a guide to the patient's problem, the helpful advice may not produce any change merely because he does not know what the advice means. He understands the words but not the idea which is beyond his present level of experience. Similarly, the general practitioner who is bombarded with too many comments may forget the majority, however helpful they may be.

It will be helpful to remember that we can provide feedback about two distinct matters – the doctor's intentions and the attempts to bring about the intentions. We are required, therefore, to understand why the consultation was as it was. This will not usually lead us to evaluate it differently but will provide us with insights to the doctor's intentions. Consider the example of a doctor who spends a considerable amount of time in a consultation exploring the possibility that a patient has a psychosexual problem underlying his physical complaint. If, at the end of the consultation, the patient has not revealed any such problem, it is possible that the problem does not exist. However skilful the doctor's attempts, the teacher may feel that they were inappropriate for that patient. If, on the other hand, the teacher feels that the patient did have a problem of this kind but that it was not discovered, he may decide that the doctor could have explored it more effectively. When any aspect of a consultation is marked down on the grounds of inappropriateness, feedback is required which is based on a clear understanding of why the doctor acted as he did. If it is marked down on the grounds of inadequacy, the doctor may need to be helped to learn new skills.

In order to ensure that feedback is always helpful and consistent with the principles we have described, we have found it necessary to state certain ground rules and to encourage all participants to keep to these rules at all times when feedback is given. Others, too, have found it necessary to control how feedback is given (Davis, Jenkins, Smail, Stott, Verby, and Wallace 1980). Our rules are as follows:

1. Briefly clarify matters of fact

It may be difficult to evaluate a consultation without access to a few crucial details such as the dose of a particular medication prescribed or whether the doctor had discussed the effects of a problem in a previous consultation. These few details should be discussed first but this is not to be used as an occasion to make points under the guise of a rhetorical question such as 'What on earth did you expect to achieve by examining the man's chest with his shirt on?'.

2. The doctor in question goes first

It is important to allow the learner to make the first comments about his consultation. The points made earlier (p. 68) should have made this matter clear. Learning will take place much more easily when the learner develops a realistic idea of his own strengths and weaknesses. What is more, the learner's remarks reveal his values and his degree of perceptiveness. The teacher needs to know about both of these matters. But it is sufficient to know that feedback is much more acceptable when the learner feels in control.

3. Good points first

In order to prevent the unhelpful spiral of attacking and defending, we insist that the learner's strengths should be discussed at length before any suggestions are made. We may think in terms of a bank account – deposits precede withdrawals. In this way we also ensure that anxiety is not raised above the minimal level which is always present when a learner allows colleagues or a teacher to observe his performance.

A doctor's investment of himself in his work is usually considerable and negative comments can be hurtful. We aim to make consultation analysis enjoyable as well as helpful, so there must be encouragement rather than punishment.

Another reason for the discussion of strengths is that the learner needs as clear an idea of what should be preserved in his consultations as he does of those aspects which could profitably be changed. Babies thrown out with bathwater might illustrate the point rather well but learning theorists would talk in terms of positive reinforcement leading to the maintenance of desirable behaviours.

There is an additional reason for discussing strengths which concerns the teacher. In observing the work of several learners the teacher will notice that their strengths and weaknesses are in different areas. The teacher needs to understand how the successful achievement of each of the tasks may be brought about. When the teacher discusses any learner's strengths in detail, he becomes familiar with possible ways in which each task may be achieved. When he notices that a learner is weak in an area in which another learner was strong, he is more able to help.

4. Recommendations not criticisms

When those tasks are discussed which were not achieved well, it is essential that recommendations should be made. Simply to inform a learner that a task was not achieved is of little help. If, on the other hand, the learner is told how he might have achieved the task, he has the opportunity of putting the matter right. But, again, we start with the learner.

It may be that the learner knows only too well which tasks he did not achieve. He may also have perfectly good ideas about how he might have achieved the task. If this is the case, the teacher does not have to be a critic at all – merely a helper. Even if the learner cannot make his own recommendations, the helping role of the teacher is still dominant when specific suggestions are made.

It may be that the teacher and the learner disagree about those tasks which were achieved well and those which were not. In this case, a discussion of criteria is needed. What criteria might we use to decide whether the effects of a problem were explored adequately and appropriately? And how might we apply these general criteria to a specific consultation with a particular patient? The teacher and the learner will need to discuss these matters and to achieve an agreement. But the discussion is part of the educational exercise. Resolution of this form of discussion may only be possible when research evidence is considered or when a more detailed examination is made of the task, the problem, the patient, the doctor and the available resources. All of these matters are usefully discussed by both learner and teacher – thus, disagreement can provoke learning too.

Learning carried out in this way is enjoyable and enjoyment of any form of learning makes it self-motivating.

The sequence of events of consultation analysis is, therefore, as follows:

1. Learner and teacher observe and usually map the consultation.
2. The learner and teacher briefly clarify any matters of fact.
3. The consultation is evaluated using the rating scale.
4. The learner discusses those tasks which, in his opinion, were achieved.
5. The teacher or other observers discuss those tasks which, in their opinions, were achieved.
6. The learner discusses those tasks which, in his opinion, were not achieved and makes any recommendations as to how these tasks might have been achieved.
7. The teacher or other observers discuss those tasks which, in their opinions, were not achieved and make their recommendations.
8. Disagreements are discussed and, if possible, resolved.
9. The learner is left with a clear summary of his strengths and of those specific changes which might lead to improvement.

Finally, it may be that a learner has to learn a completely new approach to one of the tasks. An example might be the doctor who does not know how to deal with an alcoholic or a family problem. In this case, the doctor might need to learn a new strategy for dealing with the problem in hand. On a smaller scale, the doctor might need simply to learn a new skill such as how to ask an open-ended question. The teacher will need to be able to help in the learning of both new strategies and new skills. A variety of strategies and skills has been described fully in Chapter 5. These can be developed in many ways including the provision of detailed recommendations and role play.

SUMMARY

1. Effective consulting can be learned.
2. The initial phase in the learning and teaching of effective consulting is to diagnose the learner's strengths and weaknesses.
3. In order to become more familiar with the consultation tasks and to observe each consultation closely, the consultation may be mapped on the form provided.

4. The consultation tasks can be used as criteria for evaluating a consultation. A consultation rating scale has been provided for this purpose.

5. The evaluation can be used to provide the learner with feedback.

6. Four rules must always be followed when feedback is given:

Briefly clarify any matters of fact.

The doctor in question goes first.

Good points first.

Recommendations not criticisms.

7 Educational settings

INTRODUCTION

In the previous chapters we have described an approach to learning and teaching the consultation. In this chapter we will be considering the educational settings in which this approach has been or could be applied.

UNDERGRADUATE MEDICAL EDUCATION

Wakeford (1983) reviewed the place of communication skills training in under-graduate medical schools in the United Kingdom. In a survey conducted between 1975 and 1977 he found that approximately one-third of British medical schools offered no training in communication skills; in the remainder it was normally provided within the ambit of general practice or psychiatry, and amounted to one or two hours of video recording and replay. He contrasted this with the survey by Kahn, Cohen, and Jason (1979) of United States medical schools, 96 per cent of which included courses on interpersonal skills in their curriculum. Wakeford concluded with a review of some of the difficulties and obstacles to change which are specific to medical education in the United Kingdom. Many of the factors he identifed – for example, our conservatism about existing institutions, our unwillingness to accept new ideas and the evidence of others, and our belief in the amateur rather than the professional teacher – are so pervasive that they could almost be regarded as national char-acteristics. Our experience of trying to overcome some of these obstacles in the field of vocational training will be discussed later in this chapter.

It is understandable that departments of general practice and psychiatry should devote a proportion of their curriculum time to the teaching of com-munication skills since communication is the basic clinical method of both disciplines. The danger of this, however, is that the skills and approach that are taught will be seen as only appropriate to psychiatry and general practice, rather than as relevant to the wider practice of medicine. The challenge is to distinguish between all that can be learned by undergraduates *in* general practice (for example the principles of continuing care and of prevention), in contrast to the limited amount that needs to be taught *about* general practice (for example, the organization of primary health care teams).

A number of the courses on communication skills for undergraduates in Britain have been evaluated – for example, Rutter and Maguire (1976), Pendleton and Wakeford (1979). In addition, Carroll and Munroe (1979) reviewed 36 evaluative studies, mainly of American programmes. They concluded

Instruction in clinical interviewing has, in general, promoted significant gains in students' interviewing skills, as measured by various cognitive tests, affective instruments and observed behaviour.

They identified several principles that were associated with effective programmes, including provision of direct observation and feedback on the students' interviewing behaviour, the use of carefully selected patient interviews to illustrate specific problems and the use of explicit statements of the interview skills to be learned and evaluated.

They also discussed some of the methodological problems in evaluating these courses. These problems are also relevant when we come to consider the evaluation of vocational training later in this chapter. The great majority of the programmes were short courses aimed at teaching specific skills and the research compared the skills of the same group of students before and after the course. There was no control group, however, so it is impossible to judge the effect of the other influences on the students over the same period of time. Most courses aimed to teach non-directive interviewing techniques, but there was considerable disagreement as to which specific skills constituted this overall approach. They identified the need for more research to be devoted to the observation and description of effective and ineffective interviews as determined by various measures of outcome for patients. Lastly, while many students were able to show immediate acquisition of new skills, none was able to show how long the newly acquired skills were maintained.

VOCATIONAL TRAINING FOR GENERAL PRACTICE

The approach to learning and teaching consultation skills described in this book has been developed and applied largely in the Oxford Region Vocational Training Scheme for General Practice. The approach is fundamentally different from that of teaching communication skills, however. Our approach begins by specifying aims which, taken together, form a definition of an effective consultation. This permits flexibility about how the aims are achieved. Thus, we are not interested in specifying skills *a priori* – indeed, we find it impossible to identify desirable skills without a clear idea of what we are trying to achieve. Thus, whereas the communication skills approach is prescriptive, our approach is diagnostic. We start with those tasks the learner is able to achieve and those which he cannot achieve. We offer alternative suggestions to the learner about strategies and skills which might be used to achieve those tasks which were not achieved but these suggestions are tailored to the individual's existing strengths and style. In this way, communication is seen to be inseparable from the wider context of medical practice. The communication skills approach, by contrast, runs the danger of creating a false separation which permits clinically orientated doctors to dismiss communication as of secondary importance.

The importance of the consultation for our curriculum has been recognized for a long time – in 1972 *The future general practitioner: learning and teaching,* a book reviewing the knowledge, skills, and attitudes that were essential for general practice, devoted its first two chapters to the consultation, and stated that 'the consultation is central to the whole of this report'. It is only very recently, however, that many of the vocational training schemes for general practice in the United Kingdom have started to include training in either communication skills or effective consulting in their curriculum. Hasler (1978) reviewed reports by trainees in teaching practices in the Oxford Region and found that 24 out of 54 trainees had not been observed consulting or taken part in any joint consultations throughout their years as a trainee. In 1980 trainees attending the Fourth National Training Conference at Exeter reported that on average, only 29 per cent of trainees in their general practice year had had their trainer regularly observe them consulting, although this figure hides a wide variation from 68 per cent in one region to 4 per cent in another. Why, then, is there such a large gap between intention and performance? What are the difficulties and how can they be overcome?

The first difficulty comes from the belief that communicating with patients comes naturally to doctors. It is thought that trainees, for example, will learn by experience how to handle the consultations and problems that they meet in general practice. Similarly, established doctors who did not receive any training are thought to be quite capable of conducting adequate consultations. If doctors do not observe their trainees' or colleagues' consultations or receive any feedback on their own, then these beliefs can continue unchallenged.

The second difficulty arises from the structure and organization of vocational training now enshrined by the Vocational Training Act. While the training period for general practice is nominally three years, only one year is spent attached to a trainer in general practice. Traditionally the majority of this time is spent by the trainee seeing patients, and only a small proportion is devoted either to teaching in the practice or to attending day release or residential courses outside the practice.

Thirdly, the trainer's principal responsibility continues to be the care of his own patients, and he has limited time either for teaching or for the development of his own teaching skills.

Lastly, the trainer and trainee are working closely together for a year and there is understandable concern that any criticism, particularly of anything as important as the doctor's ability to consult, could be disturbing to the relationship between them.

Trainers are not a homogeneous group, however, and their ability to adopt and adapt to new ideas varies considerably. They also share much of the conservatism of their colleagues in medical school which has been discussed above. On the other hand, vocational training schemes are relatively new and many have demonstrated their capacity to innovate, to experiment and to accept new ideas.

Becker (1982, personal communication) has identified a number of factors which influence the acceptance of innovations which he grouped under three headings:

1. The characteristics of the innovation

(a) its advantage relative to existing patterns of work;
(b) the degree of disruption to existing ideas and practices;
(c) its complexity;
(d) the degree of risk, either to the ego or to the position of the doctor, particularly if it fails;
(e) the financial or resource implications of the innovation;
(f) whether it can be introduced in manageably sized stages;
(g) the credibility of the proponents of the innovation.

2. The characteristics of the adopters

Some individuals are more likely to accept innovations than others. They tend to be relatively younger and also to frequently look outside their established local networks for new ideas.

3. The setting

The most important factor is the relationship between the decision making group and the adopting group and the degree to which the adopting group are involved in the decisions. Another factor is the group's previous experience of innovation which will also affect their readiness to adopt new ideas and practices.

If we consider in the light of these principles some of the difficulties in vocational training which have already been described we can then see some of the steps which need to be taken to introduce the teaching of effective consulting to vocational training.

The first step is to demonstrate to both trainers and trainees the need for and the value of looking critically at consultations. This can only be done by experience, not exhortation, and it is more valuable to start with volunteers who are more likely to be innovators and opinion leaders in their own groups. It is important, however, to use these individuals to involve the whole of the trainer or trainee group in discussions both on the criteria that will be used for looking at consultations and the ways that it could be included in their teaching. The rules for looking at consultations described in Chapter 6 should not, however, be negotiable, as it is important that any group's first experience of looking at consultations should demonstrate that it can be constructive rather than destructive.

In our 48-hour residential courses for trainees in the Oxford Region, early in their training year, we have included a day when trainees look at their own consultations with simulated patients. We use the approach we have described in this book and have found that this generates a desire and a demand by the trainees themselves that their consultations should be looked at in practice. We also encourage trainers and trainees to agree at the outset that looking at consultations is an essential part of the attachment and that it should begin early. This is because the longer the trainee has been consulting in general practice, the greater his investment in his own approach, and the greater the threat in having it observed and discussed.

The next step is to train trainers in the skills of observing, analysing, and commenting supportively on consultations. This can be attempted in regular trainers' meetings; as part of courses for trainers which may also look at other aspects of teaching; or on courses which are specifically designed to develop an approach to learning and teaching the consultation. One such course, organized in the Oxford Region, will be described later in this chapter.

The third step is to integrate the teaching of effective consulting into the existing structure of the vocational training scheme. As has already been described, the majority of the trainees' time is spent seeing patients in practice, and the training must be based on this experience. This is not only more economical, but also follows the educational principle that all teaching must be related to the learner's experiences and the learner must be able to relate to his future experiences what he has been taught (Freeling 1976). While some of our teaching has been based on pre-recorded tapes, particularly from the Merck, Sharp and Dohme Foundation (Pendleton and Tate 1981), or on consultations with simulated patients, the large majority has used the trainees' own consultations, recorded in their own practices.

Teaching may take place with the individual trainee and trainer, or in groups, or both. One-to-one teaching has the advantage that all the time is spent looking at the trainee's own consultations and meeting his individual needs. It can be much more immediate, and is consistent with the philosophy of vocational training that places the responsibility for monitoring the trainee's progress on the trainer. The success of the teaching, however, depends heavily in the skills of the individual trainer and on the relationship between trainer and trainee.

Teaching in small groups is more economical if teaching resources are limited, and allows trainees the opportunity of learning from each other. Balint (1957) explored the reasons for doctor's difficulties in examining psychological problems in consultations. One factor was lack of skill. He felt that the major factor, however, was doctors' avoiding personal involvement and the need for self-examination when talking to patients with problems that were often shared by the doctor. Small groups are much more effective and appropriate for examining and exploring these attitudes.

One disadvantage that particularly applies to teaching in groups, but can also affect one-to-one teaching, is that it can be episodic and repetitive, and not tailored to the trainees' developing needs. Early in the year the need may be to develop concepts of the purpose of general practice consultations and simple interviewing skills, while later in the year the trainees may wish to develop the skills of managing more complex interpersonal problems. It is helpful for the trainees' progress to be reviewed periodically through the year, and for goals then to be agreed for the next period of training.

The relative merits of different methods of observing consultations will be described in the next chapter, and our reasons for preferring the use of video recordings will also be discussed. If teaching effective consulting, based on recordings of the trainees' own consultations, is to become an integral part of a vocational training scheme, then sufficient recording equipment will need to be obtained. In the Oxford Region, we now have at least one video recorder and camera for each district scheme, which have been purchased with Section 63 funds. A decision was made early that all the equipment should be compatible. The equipment is then taken from one teaching practice to the next. It is essential that the trainers and trainees are familiarized with the way that the equipment works, as technical problems and poor quality recordings can very quickly kill initial enthusiasm.

Another problem is that while it takes a relatively short time to record a number of consultations, the process of reviewing and discussing them is much more time consuming. A number of practices have chosen to purchase their own video recorder so that this can be spread out over a longer period. If the practice also possesses a camera this increases the variety of ways in which the equipment can be used – for example, for recording repeat consultations with the same patient, or consultations which are anticipated to be either interesting or difficult. We shall discuss these and other related matters in greater detail in the next chapter.

COURSES FOR TRAINERS

The approach to learning and teaching the consultation described in this book has been used as the basis for three residential courses for trainers and other general practitioners, which together have been attended by 78 doctors, 45 of whom were trainers in the Oxford Region. The design of the three courses has been similar.

In the first session there is a factual presentation of the concepts on which the approach to the consultation and the cycle of care described in Chapter 3 is based. The consultation tasks described in Chapter 4 are then presented, and the course participants are given the opportunity of discussing them and opting in (or out) of these tasks as a basis for evaluating their own consultations. The participants are then asked to recognize the performance of these tasks in a pre-recorded consultation, using the consultation map described in Chapter 6, and lastly they are asked to evaluate the pre-recorded consultation, using the rating scale and the rules for giving feedback, also described in Chapter 6. The consultations are those of the group leaders, which helps to diffuse some of the participants' anxiety about having their own consultations observed on the following day.

The aims of the second day are to apply in practice the content of the first day, and to give the members of the course the opportunity to observe and evaluate their own consultations and those of other members of their group. The entire second day is spent in small groups, with each member in turn interviewing a simulated patient in front of the group. This is then followed by discussion and feedback, both from other members of the group and from the simulated patient. Each sequence of consultation and discussion takes 45 minutes to 1 hour, and it is therefore advantageous for each group to have no more than six members.

The simulated patients have been psychology students, members of an amateur dramatic society and, latterly, a group of professional actors ('Northwest Spanner'). Each person has been provided with a brief describing the patient and the situation they are being asked to portray. This method, which has also been described by Jason, Kagan, Werner, Elstein, and Thomas (1971) and Meadow and Hewitt (1972) has considerable advantages. The simulated patient can provide a fairly constant portrayal of the problem which can be chosen to suit the level and purposes of the course. If the actor stays in role after the end of the interview it is also possible for a learner to interview the patient again, exploring the use of different skills, after he has received feedback. More recently, we have found that using professional actors has made this even more successful, but the principle is the same for any simulator.

The greatest advantage of using simulated patients is that they are available to participate in the discussion and provide feedback themselves. The degree of achievement of a number of consultaion tasks – for example, exploring the patient's ideas and concerns, or sharing understanding – can only be assessed by reference to the patient, and the patient's reactions and response to an interview can be very different from those of other observers. This process, therefore, can increase the validity of the judgements that observers make in evaluating consultations. (Please see Appendix p. 109 for details of possible role play briefs to actors.)

During the consultations on the second day a number of the tasks will have been less well achieved than others; some of these difficulties will be inherent in the abilities of the members, while others can be predicted from the nature of the cases portrayed by the actors. The purpose of the third day is to start to consider how doctors can be helped to acquire alternative strategies and skills, as described in Chapter 5. This is a diagnostic process. The emphasis during this session is on the variety of different approaches that can be used to achieve each task and on the importance of tailoring teaching to the needs and the existing style of the individual learner.

The last session of the course is devoted to considering the ethics and the practicalities of recording consultations in practice, as described in Chapters 8 and 9.

These courses have been evaluated in a variety of ways:

1. A pre- and post-course attitude scale, the items of which have been derived from the approach to the consultation. This has demonstrated marked shifts of attitudes in the desired direction.

2. A pre- and post-course exercise in which the members of the course are invited to observe the same consultation and to write down the comments that they would like to make about the consultation if the doctor was their trainee. This has been scored for adherence to the rules of giving feedback and for the use of items from the task-rating scale. A marked increase in the participants' use of the tasks and provision of supportive feedback has been demonstrated.

3. A post-course assessment by the course members of the degree of achievement of each of the aims of the course. In all three courses the members believed that the aims had been achieved.

4. A follow-up after six-months, enquiring about the doctor's subsequent use of the approach to the consultation described on the course.

This again demonstrates the relative simplicity of evaluating the short-term effects of a brief and straightforward course. We have not sought to evaluate any changes in the course members' own consultations or the effectiveness of their teaching in practice. The difficulties of such evaluation, or, indeed, of evaluating the outcomes of our approach, either for trainees or for their patients, will be discussed more fully in Chapter 10.

CONTINUED MEDICAL EDUCATION

The principal aim of the course that has been described is to develop the members' teaching ability, and any effect that the course has on their own consultations is secondary. This does not mean that there is not an important place for established general practitioners to have the opportunity for developing and maintaining their ability to consult. Many of the studies described in previous chapters – for example, Byrne and Long (1976) and Tuckett (1982) – which demonstrated major deficiencies were studying the consultations of established doctors. Pendleton and Schofield (1983) argued the importance of feedback in maintaining doctors' motivation and performance, particularly at highly skilled tasks.

Verby *et al.* (1979) described the experience of a group of experienced principals in general practice who met regularly as peers to review audio-visual recordings of their consultations. The exercise was evaluated using a scale to rate consultations recorded at intervals of between three and five months, which showed consistently higher scores after the period of self-observation and peer review.

A number of factors, including the increasing proportion of general practitioners who had been vocationally trained, the availability of video recording
equipment, the development of approaches to looking at consultations and the
increasing interest in methods of performance review in general, all make it
likely that many more general practitioners will be involved in peer review of
their own consultations in the future. Introducing this innovation will require
many of the steps already described in the context of vocational training.

THE CASE FOR COLLABORATION

Although this chapter is about educational settings, one recurring theme is the
possible contribution of members of related disciplines. It is true that the
majority of the programmes which have been reported – for example, Maguire
and Rutter (1976), Byrne and Long (1976), Verby *et al.* (1979) and the work
reported in this volume – have involved collaboration between doctors and
behavioural scientists. In the United States, Hornsby and Kerr (1979) found
that 90 per cent of residency programmes had at least one faculty member
teaching behavioural science. Half of these were behavioural scientists; of the
doctors, half were psychiatrists.

Other disciplines can contribute to general practitioner education in a variety
of ways; the traditional method is to have members of other therapeutic
disciplines – for example, clinical psychologists – to describe their own work in
their own setting and to help the doctors make more appropriate referrals.
More recently, they have been invited to identify and teach specific skills from
their own disciplines which could be applied in the context of general practice –
for example, counselling, anxiety management training, or practice management.
For this to be of value it is essential that the behavioural scientists are familiar
with the work of general practice and that the recommendations and teaching
have been tailored to be appropriate. Behavioural scientists can also make
valuable contributions to teaching in other areas – for example, interprofessional
relationships, the exploration of attitudes, and the promotion of self-awareness
and professional growth.

The scientific contribution which can be made by other disciplines in developing doctors' understanding of the nature of their work and of their patients'
problems and behaviour is well illustrated by the first three chapters of this
book. Another major contribution which we hope is also exemplified by this
book is assistance with understanding, developing, and evaluating our methods
of teaching and learning in medical education.

We do not wish to imply that one can only teach effective consulting with the
assistance of a behavioural scientist. There is a fundamental difference, however,
between, on the one hand, being able to practise, and, on the other, understanding the concepts behind the practice. Behavioural scientists are frequently
able to discover and to understand these concepts. They may also be able to
teach well, but any doctor who wishes to become a trainer needs to learn both

to understand the principles on which his subject is based and to teach effectively. Collaboration between practitioners and behavioural scientists may help the trainers develop their teaching expertise in this way.

SUMMARY

The approach to learning and teaching the consultation described in the other chapters of this book has been applied in a variety of settings, including vocational training, undergraduate medical education, courses for general practitioner trainers and in small groups of established doctors reviewing their own consultations.

The introduction of an innovation requires attention to the characteristics of the innovation, the characteristics of the potential adopters and the setting in which the innovation is to take place.

It is particularly important to ensure that the potential trainers, teachers, and group leaders are familiar with the rationale and methods of the approach.

Plate 1. Camera placed unobtrusively in corner of consulting room with recorder under chair.

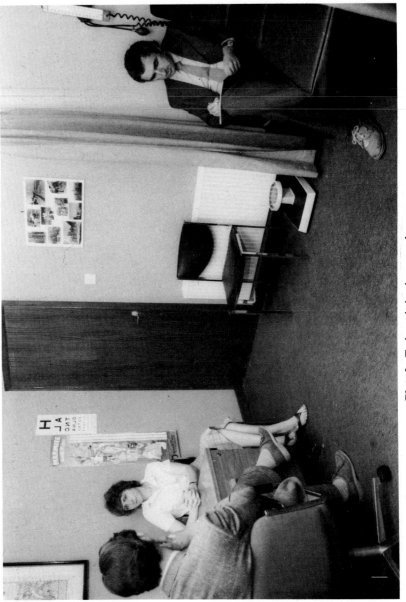

Plate 2. Trainer sitting in as an observer.

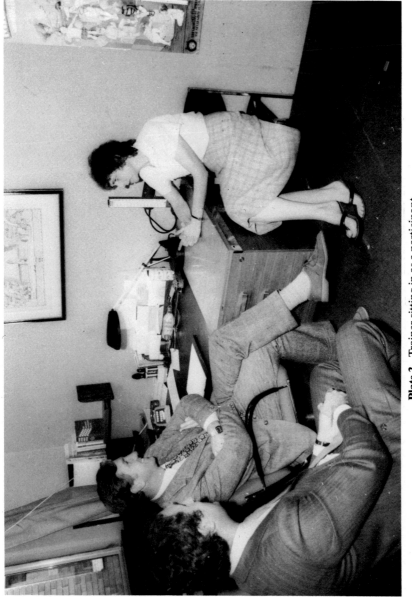

Plate 3. Trainer sitting in as a participant.

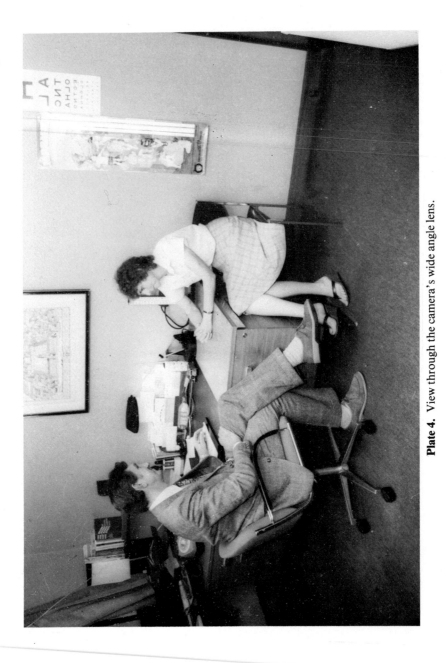

Plate 4. View through the camera's wide angle lens.

8 Methods of observing the consultation

INTRODUCTION

We have discussed the prime importance of the consultation in medical practice, and in the previous chapter we have shown that a doctor needs constructive feedback on his performance in order to improve his effectiveness in the consultation. To receive feedback the doctor must first have his consultation observed, either mechanically or by another person. We have chosen to focus on direct observation in the doctor's consulting room since we are mainly teaching trainee general practitioners who are themselves regularly consulting with their own patients and therefore feedback on consultations with role players or someone else's patients is unecessarily difficult to organize and is not as convincing initially. We appreciate that having an observer or a camera in the consulting room may affect the doctor and patient to some extent, but we endeavour to make the situation as close to a 'normal consultation' as possible.

In this chapter we would like to review those methods of direct observation that are in current use. We shall look at the advantages and disadvantages of each and give some guidance about each method.

SITTING IN

Having the learner 'sit at the master's feet' has been a part of medical teaching from the early days of Hypocrates. It is used extensively in hospital practice, in Outpatients as well as on the teaching wardround. In general practice, one of the common means of teaching, particularly at an early stage in the learner's medical career, is to sit in and watch the teacher at work, with comments and teaching normally occurring when the patient has left the room. The role reversal of the teacher sitting in and observing the learner's consultations is more difficult and much less common. It was described in 1976 by Elliott Binns, a general practitioner trainer, and two trainees (Elliott Binns, Hooker, and Willis 1976). This paper and others highlights the difficulties of sitting in. The trainer, in observing the trainee's work, often becomes involved in the consultation, either by being brought in by the trainee or the patient, or because the teacher is unable to remain silent. Although there are many good teaching points in these joint consultations, they change the trainee's normal pattern of consulting to such an extent that it is extremely difficult to use these sessions to provide feedback for the trainee. Non-involvement can be enhanced in a number of ways:

1. The chairs can be placed so that the observer is out of the field of vision of the patient consulting the trainee or learner (see Fig. 8.1).

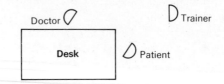

Fig. 8.1. Seating position for observation by trainer.

2. The trainer can avoid eye contact with the patient, so reducing his involvement in the consultation, although this is difficult. The trainer would find it very difficult to be anything other than a participator in this consultation (see Fig. 8.2).

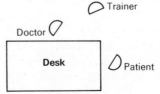

Fig. 8.2. Seating position for trainer participation.

The doctor and patient might be able to forget the presence of an observer in the consulting room if the chairs were arranged as in Fig. 8.1.

A trainer can use both seating arrangements for observation and for teaching, but he must recognize that they are different and that they have different advantages and disadvantages. When he participates he is able to discuss and demonstrate with the patient points in the history and examination that could be of interest to the trainee, but he is unable to make valid comments about the effectiveness of the trainee's consultation because of his intrusion into the usual one-to-one relationship between the patient and doctor. When a trainer observes the consultation and does not participate, he is able neither to point out the salient details in the patient's history nor demonstrate relevant features by an examination while the patient is there, but he *is* able to provide more objective feedback to the trainee about his performance in the consultation.

When sitting in, it may be difficult to decide when feedback should be given. To give feedback between consultations makes the series of consultations disjointed, emphasizes the presence of the trainer to the trainee and takes a great deal of time. It also needs to be carefully planned, or it may produce agitation amongst patient, doctor, and staff. The disadvantages of giving feedback at the end of the session, however, is that the details of the consultations might have been forgotten, and it is therefore important for the trainer to make notes and to summarize in his mind the feedback that he is going to give at the end of each consultation.

The advantages of sitting in are that it is easy to set up, needs no equipment, and is available to all trainers in practice. However, apart from the serious disadvantages that the trainer is often unable to remain uninvolved and therefore intrudes into the trainee's consultation, the learner is aware that there is another person sitting in and thinking about the consultation as it happens. This can be very off-putting. Probably the biggest disadvantage is that the trainee is unable to observe his own consultation, and all he has is his trainer's interpretations of how he performed. This can lead to difficulties unless it is treated sensitively.

THE TWO-WAY MIRROR

Because of the obtrusiveness of sitting in as a method of observation, a number of doctors have installed two-way mirrors in their surgeries, so that they can observe their trainees' consultations without disrupting them. A two-way mirror (sometimes called a one-way mirror, or one-way glass), is a piece of glass which has been coated on one side so that it appears as a mirror in the consulting room when the viewing room is darkened, and from the viewing side as a window. The two-way mirror has been used in a number of centres to demonstrate psychiatric history-taking, but only recently has it been used in the general practice setting.

The advantages and disadvantages of this method for observers have already been described (Milligan and Stewart 1981), but the most obvious advantage is the lack of disruption of the consultation by the observer. The disadvantages are that it is expensive and disruptive to the surgery premises when it is being installed. It needs a room for the observer to sit that is secure, to protect confidentiality, and there needs to be an efficient method of transmitting sound from the consulting room to the observing room. The major disadvantage still remains, however, that the trainee is unable to observe his own performance directly, and therefore any feedback that he gets is always secondhand. Figure 8.2 shows how the two-way mirror might be used.

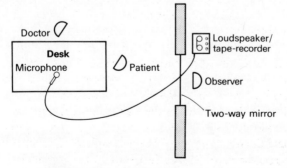

Fig. 8.3. The use of the two-way mirror.

AUDIO-TAPE AND VIDEO-TAPE

Because of the obvious need to overcome the disadvantages of the previous methods of observing consultations, other techniques were developed to provide feedback for doctors and their trainees. The first method to be adopted was the use of audio-tape – either a cassette recorder or a reel-to-reel tape recorder was used to record the consultation, which could then be played back to analyse the verbal behaviour in the consultation. A great deal of work has been done using this method, the most important being that of Byrne and Long in their book *Doctors talking to patients* (1976). They recorded on audio-tape 2500 consultations from almost 100 general practitioners in the United Kingdom, and the work they produced became the basis for much of the subsequent work on the analysis of general practice consultations. Despite the tremendous benefit derived from this work, its authors pointed out that in using audio-tape they were unable to observe non-verbal behaviour in the consultation, and they recognized this as a defect of their method. In a subsequent paper Byrne and Heath (1980) looked again at real consultations on video-tape and concluded that non-verbal behaviour is of immense importance. The importance of non-verbal communication in the general practice consultation has been demonstrated and emphasized by many authors such as Pietroni (1976), who argued that:

each general practitioner needs to be aware of his own non-verbal behaviour to become more sensitive to his patients.

There are, of course, some aspects of non-verbal behaviour in the speech of the doctor and patient (pitch, timing, accent, stress, and non-fluencies) but much more non-verbal communication is visual.

Another disadvantage of using audio-tape is that analysing behaviour in this way can be very tedious. There are large gaps of non-conversation when the doctor is writing, examining, or just listening in silence, and there is no indication of what is going on in the consultation during those times.

Recording with audio-tape

Methods

Any tape recorder can be used for recording consultations, providing it is used with a reasonably receptive microphone and is portable or unobtrusive enough to be used in the surgery. Many very worthwhile recordings have been used with small dictaphones using the integral microphone, but the sound quality is often poor. It is important, both in audio-taping and video-taping, to make the method as unobtrusive as possible, and in the case of audio-taping this means putting the tape-recorder out of sight.

In order to get the best out of a recording, the microphone, although in a position between the doctor and patient, should not be obvious. It is better not to rest the microphone directly on the desk, as it picks up the sounds of paper rustling and of movement. If possible, it is best to use a tape that runs for the full length of the surgery, so that the doctor can turn it on at the beginning of surgery and only turn it off if patients do not wish to be recorded. Finally, it is worthwhile recording the position of the tape as indicated by the digital counter on the recorder, so that specific consultations can be found easily.

Recording with video-tape

The video market is at the moment one of the most expanding markets in the United Kingdom, and this means that the equipment is now readily available and coming down in price. There are a number of different systems, as well as many different makes of recorder and camera, but the different systems have developed separately and are not compatible with each other. The most common systems in home video use are VHS and Betamax, but new systems are coming out all the time, so any recommendations we make here will need to be confirmed with a dealer. Despite this continually developing market, the following guidelines will remain useful:

1. The system should ideally be compatible with others in the postgraduate centre, trainers' group, region, home, etc., so that the same tapes can be used on all of the local machines. If possible, the camera should also be useable with all of the local machines. This is not difficult to ensure.

2. Equipment needs to be portable so that it can be moved easily. Unless the system is permanently set up in one consulting room, it has to be rugged to withstand transportation from surgery to surgery. Most of the systems sold as 'portable' will be sufficiently robust.

3. Because a lot of doctors' surgeries are small rooms, it is often very difficult to bring both doctor and patient into the field of vision of the camera, and therefore for any room with less than 5 metres between camera and subjects it is important to get a system that has a wide-angle lens. This usually means that a doctor is able to continue consulting in his own room without moving to a larger one and, since it is important for the learner to feel at ease when recording his consultations, the room he is most used to working in is the best for recording.

4. The system chosen must take an extension microphone. Most home video systems have a microphone on the camera, but in the interview setting this produces poor sound and makes listening quite difficult.

5. The newer video systems have a 'search' facility incorporated. This useful feature makes it possible to search quickly through a tape while the picture remains on the screen, to find the particular consultation, or part of the consultation that is needed. Without this facility much time is wasted trying to find a particular episode in a series of consultations.

6. The system chosen should be able to record a whole surgery without changing tapes. It is very disruptive for a doctor to run out of tape in a consultation. It makes him more conscious of the recording. Many systems have tapes

which will play for up to three or four hours but some of the more recent portable systems have introduced half-hour tapes in order to make the system smaller. These are to be avoided in favour of the three-hour tapes.

' 7. It is an advantage, but not a necessity, to have a remote control facility on the video-tape recorder, so that the tape-recorder is easily switched off from the doctor's desk if the patient does not wish to be recorded when he comes into the surgery. It produces less disruption and makes the subsequent consultation flow more easily.

8. Most modern video tape recorders and cameras record and play back in colour. This is a pleasant luxury that makes for easier watching but is not really very important.

9. The range and expense of home video systems is great, but a good-quality picture is not a necessity for giving feedback on a consultation. It is possible to use poor-quality pictures to very good effect, particularly in the training practice, so great expense on good-quality equipment is often not justified. Good sound, however, is crucial

The VTR system we want should have the features shown in Table 8.1.

Table 8.1. *Required features of a VTR system*

	Desired	Essential
Portability		– – – – – – – – – – – – – – – – X – – – – – – –
Compatibility		– – – – – – – – – – – – – – – – X – – – – – – –
Search facility		– – – – – – – – – – – X – – – – – – – – – – – –
Long-play tapes		– – – – – – – – – – – X – – – – – – – – – – – –
Wide-angle lens		– – – – – – X – – – – – – – – – – – – – – – – –
Extension microphone		– – – – – – – – – – – X – – – – – – – – – – – –
Low-light camera		– – – – – – – – – – – X – – – – – – – – – – – –
Remote control		– – X –

Setting up the video equipment

Once the equipment has been purchased it is important that the doctor is able to set up and dismantle the equipment easily and sort out any minor problems that might occur. Fear of the equipment is very infectious, and if a trainer is unable to set up and use the video equipment without anxiety, the trainee will almost certainly be unable to do so either. It is important to practise setting up the equipment and using it before recording a surgery, and to have a trial run to make sure that everything is working correctly. There is enough anxiety in the first recording of live consultations without fear of the equipment adding to the overall sense of panic. When setting up the equipment in the consulting room, the wires, cameras, microphones, and video recorder should be as unobtrusive as possible, so that they remain unnoticed by both doctor and patient.

Camera position

Camera position is important when setting up the equipment. Often the confines of the consulting room limit the choices, but if it is possible to include the facial expressions of both doctor and patient this is an advantage. If it is only possible to see one face, however, more information can be gained from the patient's expressions than from the doctor's. The camera should be set at the eye level of the seated doctor and patient. If it is placed above this, the doctor and patient are reduced in size on the picture and look somwhat unnatural. If a wide-angle lens is not obtainable it is possible to increase the field of vision of the camera by the use of a mirror as in Fig. 8.3

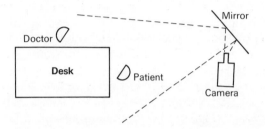

Fig. 8.3. The use of a mirror to increase the field of vision of the camera.

The camera is pointed into a mirror, thus recording a reversed image of the consultation. By this means it is possible to place the camera less obtrusively as well as to increase the field of vision in a small consulting room.

Lighting

With a modern camera it is no longer necessary to have additional lighting, though better quality pictures are obtained if there is more light in the consulting room. A low light level produces poor colour definition and 'ghosting' when either the doctor or patient move around the room. It is possible to increase the total light in the consulting room without the obtrusive use of spotlights or obvious film lighting equipment by increasing the wattage of the bulb in the existing light sockets, or by adding a standard lamp or other free-standing light with a large wattage bulb.

Most of the home video cameras now have an automatic iris control, so that if bright light shines directly into the lens the iris closes and cuts out the light. This means that bright lights behind the subjects being filmed 'dazzle' the camera and only a silhouette of the subjects is obtained. If the consultation desk is by the window it is sometimes necessary to draw the curtains in bright sunlight to prevent this from hapenning.

Sound

As we have mentioned before, most modern video cameras have a microphone on the camera and the sound level is controlled automatically. This means that the microphone is 5 metres or more away from the subjects being filmed and the sound is often distorted and incoherent. It is therefore advisable to get an extension microphone on the desk that cuts out the microphone on the camera, to produce better quality sound. It is important not to put this microphone directly in the desk, however, to prevent the rustle of papers and movements of the desk being picked up. Microphones are now being produced which are hardly larger than a thumbnail – these give excellent quality sound and are hardly noticeable by the doctor and patient.

Machine and control

In order to make the filming unobtrusive, as much of the machine and equipment as possible should be out of the direct vision of the patient. It is important, however, to have the controls of the tape recorder easily accessible so that if a patient does not wish to be video-taped the doctor can turn off the machine without fuss and avoid any embarrassment to the patient. The modern video-recorders are completely silent running, so there is no noise to intrude on the consultation. Once the equipment has been set up, the television may also be removed from the room, since it is not used in recording. When setting up the equipment it is advisable to have the tape counter in ready view so that a note can be made of the tape position at the start of each consultation. This makes it easier to find individual consultations on the tape.

Playback

The playing back of either audio or video tape recordings takes time, and it is important to give sufficient time for this. The doctor can look at his own tape and use the rating scale on his own, or playback can be with a colleague or group of colleagues. Whenever an audio or video tape is analysed, however, it is essential to remember how to give constructive feedback. The rules discussed in Chapter 6 are not to be forgotten.

SUMMARY

1. Direct observation has played a part in the teaching and learning of the consultation for many years, mainly with the observer sitting in on consultations.

2. Other methods of observation have since been developed. Of these, video-recording seems to have the most advantages (see Table 8.2).

3. For successful video-recording of consultations and useful playback, it is essential to be familiar with the equipment.

Table 8.2. *Methods of observing real consultations*

	Sitting in	One-way mirror	Audio-tape	Video-tape
Possible to replay	no	no	yes	yes
Interesting to replay	n/a	n/a	***	****
Cheap	*****	**	****	**
Easy to set up	*****	*	****	***
Easy to operate/use	**	****	****	****
Silent in use	*	yes	yes	yes
Unobtrusive	*	****	*****	****
Verbal behaviour can be observed	yes	yes	yes	yes
Non-verbal vocal behaviour can be observed	*****	*****	****	*****
Non-verbal visual behaviour can be observed	yes	yes	no	yes

9 Ethics and acceptability of video-recording

INTRODUCTION

The use of video-tape recording in the doctor's surgery has produced emotion. There have been headlines in the medical and also the national press referring to 'the spy in the surgery' and the lack of confidentiality of this method of teaching. There has even been a question in Parliament. In this chapter we shall be looking at the ethics of video-recording in the consultation; how to obtain consent for the recording; and the acceptability of the technique to patients, doctors, and the profession as a whole.

CONSENT FOR RECORDING AND USE FOR TEACHING

There is a wide range of methods currently in use for obtaining consent; they range from signed, written permission from the patient before and after the consultation to a doctor putting a notice on his waiting room saying that recording is taking place and patients may object if they wish. For a consent system that does not disrupt the doctor–patient relationship or produce risk of possible medico-legal problems and is ethically correct, we feel that it is important to adhere to the following principles:

1. There must be informed consent on every occasion of recording. There is no place for blanket permission, such as a notice in the waiting room or on a receptionist's desk, where the patient has to take the initiative in order to refuse. The best recommendation was made in an editorial in the *Journal of the Royal College of General Practitioners* in 1975, referring to the use of audio tape:

> We therefore believe that patients should always have an opportunity to discuss whether or not a consultation will be recorded and that consent should be re-sought on every occasion when a machine is used (October 1975).

2. Patients must be given every possible opportunity to refuse to have their consultation video-taped. This refusal must be made very easy, and the patient must not be made to feel that it is in any way the wrong thing for them to do, or that giving their permission is expected of them. Patients who do give their permission are in fact doing their doctor a favour.

3. The consent form must not only include permission to record the patient's consultation, but must also include permission to show the recording to other

doctors. If recordings will be shown to other groups of people, then specific permission is needed from the patient for this too.

4. The patient should always be given the opportunity to have the recording erased at the end of the consultation if he wishes, and this should also be made as easy as possible.

With these four principles in mind, there are certain practical points that should clarify the consent process.

1. The consent form should have some written explanation of what is happening and the reasons behind it.

2. The patient should understand to whom the recordings will be shown and for what purpose.

3. It is helpful, and a relief to some patients, if the examination couch is not in camera shot and they are informed of this.

4. Giving written information and gaining consent before the patients enter the consultation room leads to much less disruption to the subsequent consultation.

5. The consent procedure should be made comprehensive and easy so as not to produce anxiety in the doctor, patient, or staff before the consultation takes place.

6. The consent procedure should disrupt the normal routine of the surgery as little as possible.

With these principles and practicalities in mind it is possible to establish a consent procedure that is acceptable to doctors, patients, and staff. One of us (PBH) uses the following system: on reporting to the reception desk, the patient is informed that the surgery is being video-taped and is given the opportunity of refusing to have his consultation filmed. He is given a consent form providing information about the procedure (see Appendix 2), which he is asked to read and on it to indicate by signing, whether or not he wishes to be recorded. He is then asked to hand the form to the doctor on entering the consulting room, and the doctor confirms by looking at the form that consent has been given. If consent is refused the video-recorder is switched off without discussion or need for justification, and the consultation continues without disruption. There are, of course, a number of variations on this and the consent procedure may need to be adapted to meet the requirements of each doctor in his own surgery.

PATIENTS' VIEWS ON VIDEO-RECORDING

There have been a number of descriptions of video-recording in the consultation, and patients' reactions to some of these have been sought. Papers such as that of Taylor (1977) and Campbell (1982) confirm our own experience that with adequate explanation and consent, very few patients have any objection to the recording of their consultations. We found, in line with published surveys, that only about one patient in ten does not wish to have his consultation recorded. There seems to be no consistent feature of either the patients who refuse or their subsequent consultations – there is no sex or age bias, no subject common to the consultations and the patients are no more or less concerned about their problems. It just seems that some patients at some times do not wish to have their particular consultations recorded.

The rate of refusal diminishes still further if the doctor is experienced with and not apprehensive about the technique. A smooth, informative, and trouble-free consent system reduces the patients' apprehension, and this increases the acceptability of the technique. The fullest survey of patients' views (Campbell 1982) asked 150 patients for their reactions after video-recording their consultations, The results are shown in Table 9.1.

Table 9.1. *Patients' reactions to being video-recorded*

1.	Did the filming make you feel uneasy?	Yes = 5%
2.	Were there things that you would have told the doctor if you had not been filmed!	Yes = 2%
3.	Did you behave differently because you were being filmed?	Yes = 1%
4.	Did the doctor behave differently because he was being filmed?	Yes = 3%

Those patients who answered 'Yes' to question 4 were asked in what way the doctor behaved differently, and all replied that the doctor was more attentive than usual.

It can be seen from these results that video-recording consultations in the surgery is acceptable to the majority of patients, and that the subsequent consultations are largely unaltered by the presence of the video camera.

THE DOCTOR'S VIEW OF VIDEO-RECORDING

Over the past few years we have introduced many general practice trainees and principals – both trainers and doctors not involved in training – to the delights of seeing themselves on video. Nearly all of these doctors were very apprehensive about the experience beforehand. It must be remembered that, while there is anxiety about the recording of consultations, apprehension is probably greater about showing the recording to a group of peers. The level of anxiety is in some cases set by previous destructive and hurtful criticism, and this only serves to emphasize the rules referred to in Chapter 6. The feeling of apprehension is felt by the majority of doctors, as was shown by the survey of 41 undergraduate and postgraduate doctors shown in Table 9.2 (Davis *et al.* 1980).

These results are in line with our experience over the last four years of using video-taped consultations in the Oxford Region: once the doctor has experienced the video camera in his consulting room and has recognized the value of constructive feedback about his consulting skills, he is only too happy to agree to repeat the exercise. There is, then, surely an important message here for those apprehensive Doubting Thomases – try it and see!

Table 9.2. *Doctors' reactions to being video-recorded*

	Before first recording	After recording
Happy to agree	15	34
Apprehensive	22	7
Had grave doubts	4	0

THE PROFESSION'S VIEW OF VIDEO-RECORDING

There has been little informed comment on video-recording from the medical profession as a whole, but there have been a number of articles and comments in the popular medical newspapers. These have generally either referred to individuals who have used video-recording without the written consent of the patients, or have been written by doctors who have not had experience of the technique. The use of video-recording in the consulting room is, however, increasing in leaps and bounds; it is used in many vocational training schemes, undergraduate departments of general practice, and in continuing education for general practice principals.

The video-recording and analysis of consultations also plays a major part in the project 'What Sort of Doctor?' (Royal College of General Practitioners 1981c). This is a scheme to promote the review of a doctor's work and practice and the provision of constructive feedback about his performance. The medical profession in general, and general practice in particular, although intitially guarded about the technique, seem now to be giving their approval to video-recording of consultations for both learning and teaching purposes.

THE LAW'S VIEW OF VIDEO-RECORDING CONSULTATIONS

As far as we know, the issue of video-recording consultations for teaching purposes has not come to court in the United Kingdom or anywhere else in the world, but the fear that the recordings might be used in a way that could be detrimental to either patient or doctor is with all of us who are involved in this work. The issues involved have been reviewed well by Geertsma (1969), who comes to the same conclusion as that reached by the RCGP in 1975 – namely, that the best protection against legal action is the same that is required morally. Written consent from a well-informed patient is the best defence against criticism, both legal and moral.

There is further guidance on this matter as a result of a written parliamentary question in March, 1982, from Dr R. G. Thomas, MP for Carmarthen, to the Secretary of State for Social Services. Dr Thomas asked if the Secretary of State would take steps to prevent the video-taping of private consultations between patients and medical practitioners, and the use of such recordings for whatever purposes, including the teaching of general practitioners, so as to maintain patients' confidentiality and to prevent sound recordings of consultations, except where the patient expressly agrees to these being made.

The Secretary of State, Mr Kenneth Clarke, replied:

Recording consultations between patients and medical practitioners is an increasingly important and useful method of teaching certain aspects of medical practice, and is controlled by the ethical consideratons of patients' consent and confidentiality. I would expect any recordings of consultation to be made and put to subsequent use only with the patient's full knowledge and consent and as far as I am aware, this is invariably the case.

SUMMARY

1. Informed consent for video-recording of consultations and the use of these recordings for teaching should be freely given and in writing on each occasion.

2. Patients in general find the technique acceptable. Only 5–10 per cent refuse to have their consultations video-taped.

3. The majority of doctors are apprehensive before being recorded, but this is greatly reduced after they have experienced the technique.

4. Video-recording consultations is becoming an acceptable part of teaching general practice at all levels.

10 Unresolved issues

INTRODUCTION

In earlier chapters we have set out several arguments. We have provided a definition of an effective consultation which is based on a considerable amount of evidence. We have described ways in which a doctor might learn to practise in this way and to teach others so to do. We have also outlined some of our experiences of using this approach in a variety of settings. Our initial reason for writing this book, however, was the enthusiasm we felt about our approach to the consultation. Because of our wish always to produce a coherent argument, we have stated our case fully, and, we hope, carefully. We recognize, however, that some of the enthusiasm felt by ourselves and others may have been masked by the careful statement of our case.

Our work has resulted in collaboration between general practice and behavioural science. In 1978 we began our work by trying to apply the techniques of social skills training, unaltered, to general practice, but this did not work, as there are unique features of a consultation which distinguish it from other conversations. We needed a bespoke method, rather than something off-the-peg. We therefore had to construct our own approach, based on the two backgrounds, and this has produced a shared view of general practice, shared methods and shared values. We feel strongly that we would not have been able to develop our project to this stage without such interdisciplinary collaboration.

We have written our book now because we feel that there is a need for a coherent approach to looking at the consultation, but in publishing our ideas we are well aware that a number of aspects lack strict empirical support. Many general practitioners have now used the techniques we have described and have in this way produced a kind of validation, but empirical support will require enormous amounts of time, resources, and money. This work needs to be done, however, and we shall set out some of the main questions which need to be answered in this way, but we would like to commend our ideas as they have already been found to be useful by a large number of people.

Those aspects of our work which are still unresolved are:
1. Does achieving the tasks bring about the outcomes we predict?
2. Does consulting in this way achieve other outcomes?
3. What is happening now in general practice consultations?
4. What factors maintain this style of consulting?
5. How can doctors and patients be persuaded to change their style of consulting when necessary?

6. Is our approach to the consultation applicable to the changes which are likely in the future?

DOES ACHIEVING THE TASKS BRING ABOUT THE OUTCOMES THAT WE PREDICT?

In order to decide the ways in which effective consulting can be achieved, we have argued backwards from outcomes that we have considered to be desirable. In the earlier chapters we have presented the evidence that links the content of consultations with the desirable outcomes but we now need to prove this relationship empirically for our approach *as a whole*. We should not underestimate, however, the enormity of this suggestion.

The assumption that our tasks derive from the arguments presented in Chapter 3 can be tested by the analysis of the arguments themselves. But the more important matter concerns the effects of this style of practice.

We have attempted to put together a series of tasks which ensure that the doctor's roles in the diagnosis and management of patients' problems are given their place alongside his roles in care and support, in patient education, and in prevention. We have maintained that this combination of activities should result in patients who are better informed about their health; who look after themselves better; who follow more closely the (jointly made) decisions concerning their health; and who make better use of medical services by caring for their own health problems as appropriate. It may be, however, that there are also costs involved for patients who are deprived of the anxiety-reducing effects of a powerful healer. These matters require investigation.

To demonstrate the relationship between the achievement of the tasks and the outcomes of the consultation is a major problem. There would need to be a large number of doctors in a study of which a sizeable group would have to consult in the way we have described. We would also need to:

(i) have reliable judgements of the extent to which the tasks were achieved in observed consultations;

(ii) check the validity of these judgements with the doctors and patients themselves where appropriate;

(iii) have reliable and valid measurements of the outcomes of the consultations. The size of this study would be considerable and many methodological problems would need to be overcome.

DOES CONSULTING IN THIS WAY ACHIEVE OTHER OUTCOMES?

We need an equivalent investigation of the effects on doctors of this method of practice. It might be predicted that one consequence for doctors would be a reduction in the stresses they experience when attempting to take on the responsibility for their patients' health, but it may be that the experience of power is an important element of their job satisfaction which would be lost.

There is also the unanswered question, 'Will it all take more time?'. In the short term it probably will, but we are unable to tell whether time will be saved in the long term. It might be that this mode of practice would lead to a reduction in workload, as patients become increasingly able to look after their health. It may be, however, that this hope, which was part of the optimism which accompanied the beginnings of the National Health Service, will prove to be as forlorn on the small scale as it has been on the large scale. It may be that patients no longer present with a headache, but with the unsatisfactory home life which has caused the headache, and this will have the effect that the doctor no longer has the option of turning a deliberately blind eye to the aetiology in dealing with the symptom alone. We would argue that this leads to the practice of more appropriate medicine, but we cannot decide the effect on workload of this approach to the consultation without more extensive investigation.

WHAT IS HAPPENING NOW IN GENERAL PRACTICE CONSULTATIONS?

In Chapter 3 we set out a rationale for our seven consultation tasks. Some of them, we suggested, are not controversial – the doctor is expected, for example, to define patients' problems and to make recommendations about the management of those problems. All doctors are taught to take a medical history and to make initial decisions about the aetiology of a problem. Similarly, all doctors are instructed in the use of drugs and are familiar with other therapies. It might be expected, therefore, that the tasks which deal with these matters will be attempted in most consultations. On the other hand, the seeking of patients. beliefs about their problems is much more controversial and it might be expected that this behaviour would be in evidence far less often.

We do not know the frequency with which our tasks are attempted. To find out would require simple descriptive research. Our experience of taking part in vocational training and of other courses designed specifically for the discussion of the consultation has led us to believe that it is in the area of the doctor's educational and preventive roles that there is least activity. We have frequently noticed doctors attempting to define the nature and history of patients' problems and trying to decide on the cause. We have also seen management planned, although the typical pattern is for the doctor to make the decisions and present them to the patient, rather than to share the decision making process with the patient. We have rarely seen doctors spontaneously seek patients' ideas, however, or even seek to achieve a shared understanding of the problem with the patient.

There is certainly empirical evidence in support of our impressions (Byrne and Long 1976; Tuckett 1982), but we cannot state categorically that our impressions are accurate. It would be useful to establish how often the various tasks are attempted and how often they are satisfactorily achieved – this would help us to plan our training courses much more appropriately, although it would not help in the training of individual doctors, since this training is always tailored to the learner's own strengths and weaknesses.

WHAT FACTORS MAINTAIN THIS STYLE OF CONSULTING?

In Chapter 3 we looked at the cycle of care as it affects patients. We reviewed the literature about short- and long-term outcomes of consultations with regard to the patient. There is an equivalent cycle of care for doctors, however, with inputs to the consultation and with outcomes in both the short and long term (Pendleton 1983). There has been very little work published about the effects of consultations on doctors, but if it were possible to find out what produced a satisfactory consultation for a doctor, for example, we would know better what maintains his behaviour in the consultation.

The irony of this state of affairs is worthy of comment. First, there are considerable difficulties in investigating patient satisfaction – patients do not readily criticize or even discriminate effectively between consultations with their doctor. For this reason the investigation of the nature of patient satisfaction and the factors which can influence it is a matter which is fraught with method-oligical difficulties. Doctors, on the other hand, are much more willing to offer a variety of comments about their consultations. This has an important consequence for researchers – namely, that it is easier to identify the factors which determine doctor satisfaction than those which determine patient satisfaction (Pendleton 1981).

Secondly, there is a great deal of advice given to doctors on how to increase patient compliance. This advice is increasingly aimed at discovering those factors which maintain patients' present unhealthy behaviour and their health beliefs, and at influencing those beliefs. Ironically, there is little knowledge of those factors that maintain doctors' behaviour or increase their adherence to their stated aims. For example, there has been strong evidence for many years supporting the active prevention of cervical cancer, but where is the resistance to the programme? It has been demonstrated (Havelock 1983) that the beliefs of doctors produce resistance to the setting up of active screening projects. If doctors' beliefs inhibit this proven preventive activity, how much resistance will there be to innovations such as are suggested in this book? If doctors are to be persuaded that the approach to the consultation we are advocating is helpful, we shall need to know more about their own beliefs and feelings concerning their work and the social and other pressures which play a part in determining their present behaviour.

On our courses we pay careful attention to the participants' experience of general practice and we take care to provide them with opportunities for considering our approach and their reactions to it. But if this is needed on small-scale residential courses, how much more necessary will it be when any new initiative is offered for publication? New initiatives are to be welcomed. Advice which will genuinely help to define and produce more effective consultations and promote health to greater effect must be heard. But these initiatives will probably founder unless they can be more firmly built on an understanding of the factors which maintain present behaviour.

HOW CAN DOCTORS AND PATIENTS BE PERSUADED TO CHANGE THEIR METHOD OF CONSULTING?

The first part of this issue concerns the extent to which any doctor's present behaviour can be changed. This is tantamount to asking to what extent our teaching methods are effective. We have evaluated the effect of our training courses on teachers (see Chapter 7). It would seem that the behaviour of teachers can be influenced – they learn to use the tasks we have described when evaluating a consultation, to make their feedback positive. They also undergo a change in their attitudes. We have not done a long-term study of the effects of the training on the consulting behaviour of the participating general practitioners.

We need to know the extent to which behaviour in the consulting room can be influenced by the educational package we have described. Verby *et al.* (1979) have demonstrated the short-term effects of video-feedback on the consulting behaviour of experienced general practitioners. To investigate the influence on vocational trainees is a difficult problem as there are many influences on a trainee during his trainee year and considerable change is to be seen (Freeman and Byrne 1976; Freeman, Roberts, Metcalfe, and Hillier 1982). Properly to measure the effect of our educational package would require a control group.

As well as measuring the effects of this approach on doctors' behaviour, there is a need to assess the change in attitudes of the doctors. Our experience of using this approach leads us to believe that doctors who take on this method of consulting will have or develop positive attitudes towards the promotion of health rather than merely the treatment of disease. This, too, needs to be evaluated.

There is also the matter of the effects of this approach on undergraduates in medical schools. It is often maintained by those with responsibility for vocational training that much of their time is spent encouraging the trainees to unlearn the attitudes learned in medical school and to redirect their skills. We would argue that this remedial effort would not be needed if undergraduates were to learn to consult in this way. One major hurdle to the introduction of this form of consulting would be pressure on curriculum time but if a doctor cannot consult effectively, what use is extensive medical knowledge?

For patients, too, there will be a need to change their method of consulting if they are going to obtain maximum benefit from a doctor who practises as we are suggesting. Patients will need to come to the doctor prepared to be equal negotiating partners with their doctors – prepared to share in making decisions and to ask questions. The doctor will certainly be one major influence towards this new style of patient behaviour. Patients will learn that their doctor will expect questions, that he needs to know their ideas, concerns, and expectations and that he wishes to discuss decisions with them. Each consultation conducted in this way will influence the next, and so on. Perhaps patients need a training manual too – 'How to get the best out of your doctor'. This could be our next project.

IS OUR APPROACH TO THE CONSULTATION APPLICABLE TO THE PROBABLE OR POSSIBLE CHANGES IN GENERAL PRACTICE IN THE FUTURE?

To some extent our approach is a response to changes which have already taken place. Examples of these changes include the diminished importance of infectious diseases for which the doctor had a ready answer and the predominance of degenerative disorders which can, at best, only be prevented. We also now live in a less authoritarian, more consumer-orientated society. These trends are likely to continue, but the future may produce new challenges.

There are two views of the future of general practice that have been put forward recently. The first, by Marshall Marinker (1981) suggests that the rapid expansion of technology will give patients increasing access not only to medical facts, but also to medical decision-making facilities. Patients will, through their television at home, have access to self-diagnostic procedures provided by computers. This will make many of the mysteries of medical decision making available to the majority of the population. Patients will come to their doctor with much more information, more ideas and a wish to negotiate their management from an informed viewpoint. The general practitioner of the future will need to be able to meet this increase in consumerism.

Another vision of the future is expressed by David Metcalfe (1982), who sees general practice as the interface between rigid, high-technology hospital medicine and a fluid, ever-changing society. This means that the general practitioner always needs to be flexible to cope with this change and to be receptive to the differing views and opinions of his practice population.

These developments might bring about a radical change in the distribution of power between doctor and patient, but the fundamental needs of patients are unlikely to change. The general practitioner of the future will always need to be able to cope with patients' fears, with bereavement and with terminal illness. He will also have a part to play in bridging the gap between knowing about health and actively looking after it.

But will the doctor–patient relationship be able to cope with the possible erosion of medical expertise by an increasingly informed layman? Surely, what is now needed is an alternative value system which asserts that patients must be informed about their health and must share in making decisions with the doctor. In this way, we can anticipate one likely development and thereby enhance the relationship, rather than fight a rearguard action against the likely changes which the future will bring about.

CONCLUSION

In this last chapter we have tried to look critically at our own work. We have raised some of the issues which are still unresolved, and we are sure that there are many more. We hope that some of the enjoyment and enthusiasm that we experience in the teaching and learning of our approach is conveyed to the reader, and that you will go and try the methods for yourself.

Appendix 1
Suggested role-plays

1. MARY WELLBELOVED, aged 22

Instructions to role-player

You are a waitress. You have had a sore throat since yesterday evening and have insisted upon an urgent appointment at the end of a morning surgery. You are planning to go on holiday in three days. You do not feel unwell, and have no other problems.

Your previous doctor has always given you penicillin for your sore throats and you have always recovered in three to four days. You do not believe that aspirin cures sore throats. You fear that a sore throat might interfere with your holiday.

Instructions to doctor

This patient has just joined your list and has asked for an urgent appointment at the end of Tuesday morning's surgery.

Instructions to course organizer

This role-play explores in particular:

(1) the doctor's ability to achieve a shared understanding of the problem with the patient;

(2) the doctor's ability to decide and to plan appropriate management with the patient;

(3) the doctor's ability to establish a helpful relationship with the patient.

In this case, the definition of a helpful relationship might profitably be explored.

2. JOHN HOWARD, aged 42

Instructions to role-player

You are a bricklayer, and have applied to buy your council house with a mortgage. You are married and have two boys, aged 16 and 18.

You were asked some weeks ago to attend for a medical in connection with your mortgage application. Before you came for the medical you have not seen a doctor for five years, and have had no serious illnesses.

You have always thought of your self as very fit and do not like the idea of seeing doctors or taking tablets.

If asked, your beliefs about high blood pressure are that it is caused by stress, and that the most important thing for you to do, should you have high blood pressure, would be to take things easy and to become physically less active. You have heard that people with high blood pressure get strokes, as did your father when he was 50.

Instructions to doctor

You have been away from the practice for a month. Your partner has seen this patient on three occasions in that time, following an initial insurance medical. The patient's blood pressure has been consistently raised (more than 160 over 105) and it is raised again today. The appropriate examinations and investigations have been conducted and have been found to be normal. The decision as to whether or not to treat this patient has now to be made as he is your patient.

Instructions to course organizer

This role-play explores in particular the following:

(1) the doctor's ability to elicit the patient's ideas and concerns;

(2) the doctor's ability to achieve a shared understanding of a problem with the patient in the areas of:

  (i) the nature and history of the problem,

  (ii) implications of the problem for the patient's life,

  (iii) appropriate actions the patient should take.

(3) The doctor's ability to check the patient's understanding of and commitment to the management which has been planned.

3. MISS SALLY JONES, aged 20

Instructions to role-player

You are a third-year student at a catering college. You live at home with your mother. You haven't found a job yet and think you will have to move away from home, but are worried about leaving your mother.

The problem that you present to the doctor is headaches. You describe them as 'tight' or 'bursting', 'worse at the front and the back'. You sometimes feel sick and have to lie down. They usually come on towards the end of the day, but sometimes you wake with them, and then you miss college. They come two or three days a week.

You think these headaches are migraines. You have taken Paracetomol but they don't help much. You don't like the idea of taking tablets regularly.

If asked about headaches or migraine in the family, you will say that your father had them, but only if the doctor is very sympathetic or questions you specifically on the matter will you admit that your real concern is that your father died when you were 12 with a sub-arrachnoid cerebral haemorrhage, and you are afraid that this may happen to you.

You have a boyfriend with whom you sleep, but you are not on the Pill. You smoke, and believe that it is dangerous to take the Pill if you are a smoker. All your friends smoke and you think it would be difficult to give up.

You have no other continuing problems.

Instructions to doctor

This patient has just joined your list and you have never seen her before.

Instructions to course organizer

The doctor has not seen this patient before and the records only contain child-hood illnesses. If the doctor wishes to examine this patient he will find nothing of note – all examinations performed will be normal.

This role-play examines in particular the following:

(1) the doctor's ability to establish the nature and history of the problem;

(2) the doctor's ability to explore the patient's ideas, concerns, and expectations;

(3) the doctor's ability to identify the patient's risk factors;

(4) the doctor's ability the plan appropriate management with the patient;

(5) the doctor's ability to deal with the patient's inappropriate ideas and to establish a shared understanding of the problem with the patient.

4. SYLVIA SMITH, aged 30

Instructions to role-player

You are married to a schoolteacher and have two children, aged 8 and 6. You feel sick in the mornings. Initially you will say that you think it is unlikely that you are pregnant because you have a coil fitted, but if questioned, will admit that you missed your period 3 weeks ago and that your breasts feel a little uncomfortable. Deep down, you think you are pregnant.

Your initial concern is that you may not be able to afford to have another child, as you have now started working as a teacher again yourself. Your underlying concern, which you will only admit if questioned sympathetically, is that you would be happy to keep the child, whereas your husband would not. You would not wish to cause trouble by not doing what your husband wishes, and are reluctant to involve him with the doctor. You say that you would want to be considered for a termination. If you are not asked, you can raise this by saying 'What will happen if I am pregnant?'.

You expect the doctor will determine whether or not you are pregnant, either by examination or by a pregnancy test. Ideally, you would like the doctor to talk this matter through with you at some length.

Instructions to doctor

This patient has just joined your list and you have never seen her before.

Instructions to course organizer

If the doctor proposes an examination of the patient the signs are equivocal. If the doctor chooses to terminate this consultation promptly, while awaiting a pregnancy test, he should be asked immediately to conduct the subsequent consultation, when the positive results of the pregnancy test are returned.

This role-play explores in particular the following:

(1) the doctor's ability to define the nature and history of the patient's problem in physical, psychological and social terms;

(2) the doctor's ability to explore the patient's ideas, concerns, and expectations;

(3) the doctor's ability to achieve a shared understanding of the problem with the patient;

(4) the doctor's ability to plan appropriate management with the patient.

Discussion of this role-play should include the danger of colluding with the patient against the husband, and how a joint consultation with the husband might be handled.

5. EDWARD FRENCH, aged 30

Instructions to role-player

You are a marketing executive for a confectionery company, and are married to a dentist, but have no children.

You have just joined a new practice, and have phoned in for the tablets you usually receive, but the receptionist has asked you to see the doctor, having explained that in this practice the doctor prefers to see a new patient, rather than issue prescriptions over the phone. You feel angry at the inconvenience caused to your busy work schedule. The tablets which you have requested are Valium, 5 mg, which you normally got on repeat prescription from your previous doctor. You expect the doctor to give you a repeat prescription quickly, and are fairly impatient if this new doctor is slow or reluctant to do so.

Your symptoms are that your hands are sometimes shaky, particularly in the morning, and the reason you want the tablets is that they help to steady your hands. If questioned, you will admit that you are under a fair amount of pressure at work. Your ideas are that your tension is causing your symptoms and you are concerned that without your tablets you will not be able to cope at work.

You are very defensive about your home and sex life, but you have been married for 5 years and have not yet had any children. You are drinking regularly every lunchtime and evening, but are very defensive about it.

If the doctor suggests you have a drink problem you will initially resist this explanation. You have no other problems.

Instructions to doctor

This patient has just joined your list. You have never seen him before. He phoned in for a prescription of Valium, 5 mg × 50 – the receptionist, in line with your practice policy, explained that you would be unwilling to prescribe this medication without a consultation, and has asked the patient to see you.

Instructions to course organizer

This role-play explores in particular the following:

(1) the doctor's ability to identify the aetiology of a problem, especially the doctor's awareness of alcohol problems;

(2) the doctor's ability to achieve a shared understanding of the problem with the patient;

(3) the doctor's ability to plan management with the patient with respect to:

 (i) the repeat prescription of Valium;

 (ii) the patient's responsibility for the control of alcohol,

 (iii) the continued contact and relationship between this doctor and patient.

(4) the doctor's ability to handle an aggressive patient with different expectations from the doctor.

6. MRS ANGELA BRADLEY, aged 55

Instructions to role-player

You are a housewife with three children, all of whom have left home. Your husband is a busy executive. You have not seen this doctor before, though you have been in the area for a year. The only record that he has is of your hysterectomy which you had two years ago because of heavy bleeding. You had a check-up in hospital two months ago, and everything was perfectly all right. You do not smoke.

You have come to ask for hormone replacement therapy, and expect to be given it. Your problem is that you have frequent hot flushes and you also feel tired all the time and tearful when you are on your own. You find it difficult to get things done in the house and if asked, you wake early. You also have a dry vagina, and intercourse is painful and very infrequent. Your concerns are the effect you are having on your husband. You feel that at this stage in your life you should be able to enjoy yourselves together, but you don't enjoy anything and he has become extremely impatient. You suspect that he is staying away at work more than is strictly necessary.

Your ideas, which you are more reluctant to express, are that your tiredness is due to cancer. Your mother had cancer of the breast and died very painfully.

A number of your friends had hormone replacement therapy and you have read articles in magazines which say that it works. You also know that some doctors are reluctant to prescribe it, but your husband is very insistent that you have this treatment, and if your doctor refuses he has said that he will arrange for you to go to a private clinic.

Instructions to the doctor

This patient has just joined your list. The only significant record in her notes is of a hysterectomy for fibroids two years ago.

Instructions to course organizer

This role-play explores in particular the following:

(1) the doctor's ability to establish the physical, psychological, and social dimensions of the problem, and their contribution to its aetiology and its effects;

(2) the doctor's ability to achieve a shared understanding of the problem with the patient;

(3) the doctor's ability to plan appropriate management for the problem with the patient.

You might also wish to explore what 'appropriate management' means in this context, considering the available options which include hormone replacement therapy, anti-depressant therapy, social support, and counselling.

Appendix 2
Video-recorded consultations — patient's consent form

CONSENT TO VIDEO-RECORDED CONSULTATIONS

We would like your permission to video-record your consultation with your doctor today. No intimate examinations will be recorded.

The recording may be used afterwards to help with general practitioner teaching. It will only be seen by other doctors.

If, after the consultation, you would prefer to have the consultation erased, you may ask the receptionist before you leave.

Please will you complete this form and return it to the receptionist *before* you see your doctor.

EITHER   I agree to my consultation with my doctor today being video-recorded. I understand that it may be seen afterwards by other doctors. I also understand that I can ask for the recording to be erased after the consultation.

OR   I would prefer not to have my consultation recorded.

Signed ....

Date ....

References

Argyle, J.M. (1969). *Social interaction*. Methuen, London.
—— Furnham, A.F., and Graham, J.G. (1981). *Social situations*. Cambridge University Press.
—— and Kendon, A. (1967). The experimental analysis of social performance. In *Advances in experimental social psychology,* Vol. 3 (ed. L. Berkowitz). Academic Press, New York.
Bain, D.J. (1976). Doctor-patient communication in general practice consultations. *Medical Education* **10**, 125–31.
—— (1977). Patient knowledge and the content of the consultation in general practice. *Medical Education* **11**, 347–50.
Balint, E. and Norell, J.S. (1973). *Six minutes for the patient*. Tavistock, London.
Balint, M. (1957). *The doctor, his patient and the illness*. Pitman, London.
Barofsky, I. (1980). *The chronic psychiatric patient in the community*. Plenum, New York.
Becker, M.H. (1979). Understanding patient compliance: the contributions of attitudes and other psychosocial factors. *New directions in patient compliance*. (ed. S. Cohen). Lexington Books, New York.
—— (1982). Social science perspectives on patient compliance. Paper presented at conference, Social science and primary care. University of Oxford.
—— Haefner, D.P., Kasl, S.V., Kirschi, J.P., Maiman, L.A., and Rosenstock, I.M. (1977). Selected psychosocial models and correlates of individual health-related behaviours. *Medical Care* **15**, Suppl., 27–46.
—— and Maiman, L.A. (1975). Sociobehavioural determinants of compliance with health and medical care recommendations. *Medical Care* **13**, 10–24.
Berne, E. (1964). *Games people play*. Penguin, Harmondsworth.
The Black Report (1980). *Inequalities in health*. Department of Health and Social Security, London.
Boreham, P. and Gibson, D. (1978). The informative process in private medical consultations: a preliminary investigation. *Social Sci.* **12**, 409–16.
Brown, E.W. and Harris, T. (1978). *Special origins of depression*. Tavistock, London.
Brown, K. and Freeling, P. (1976). *The doctor–patient relationship*. Churchill Livingstone, Edinburgh.
Byrne, P.S. and Heath, C. (1980). Practitioners' use of non-verbal behaviour in real consultations. *Jl. R. Coll. gen. Practrs* **30**, 327–31.
—— and Long, B.E.L. (1976). *Doctors talking to patients*. HMSO, London.
Campbell, E.J.M., Scadding, J.G., and Roberts, R.S. (1979). The concept of disease. *Br. med. J.* **ii**, 757–62.
Campbell I.K. (1982). Audio-visual recording in the surgery: do patients mind? *Jl R. Coll. gen. Practrs* **32**, 548–9.
Carrol, J.G. and Munroe, J. (1979). Teaching medical interviewing: a critique of educational research and practice. *J. med. Education* **54**, 498–500.
Cartwright, A. and Anderson, R. (1981). *General practice revisited*. Tavistock, London.
Chamberlain, E.N. (1936). *Symptoms and signs in clinical medicine*. Wright, Bristol.
Child, D. (1973). *Psychology and the teacher*. Holt, Rinehart and Winston, London.

Coope, J. and Metcalfe, D. (1979). How much do patients know? *Jl R. Coll. gen. Practrs* **29**, 482–8.

Davis, R.H., Jenkins, M., Smail, S.A., Stott, N.C.H., Verby, J., and Wallace, B.B. (1980). Teaching with audio-visual recordings of consultations. *Jl R. Coll. gen. Practrs* **30**, 333–6.

Dunbar, J. (1979). Issues in assessment. In *New directions in patient compliance* (ed. S. Cohen). Lexington Books, New York.

Elliott Binns, C.P., Hooker, A.N., and Willis, A.W. (1976). Seeing 2 doctors at once in general practice. *Jl R. Coll. gen. Practrs* **26**, 684–6.

Elstein, A.S., Shulman, L.S., and Sprafha, S.A. (1978). *Medical problem solving: an analysis of clinical reasoning.* Harvard University Press, Cambridge, Mass.

Engel, G.L. (1971). The deficiencies of the case presentation as a method of clinical teaching. *New Engl. J. Med.* **284**, 20–4.

FDA (Food and Drug Administration) (1979). Prescription drug products: patient labelling requirements. In *Federal Register* **44**, 40016–41.

Fink, D.L. (1976). Tailoring the consensual regimen. In *Compliance with therapeutic regimens* (ed. D. L. Sackett and R. B. Haynes). Johns Hopkins University Press, Baltimore.

Fleming, D.M. (1982). Workload review. Birmingham Research Unit RCGP. *Rl Coll. gen. Practrs* **32**, 292–7.

The Fourth National Trainee Conference, Exeter 1980. Royal College of General Practitioners, London (1981).

Freeling, P. (1976). The Nuffield courses for course organisers. *Update* **13**, 1327–31.

—— (1983). The doctor–patient relationship in diagnosis and treatment. In *Doctor-patient communication* (ed. D. A. Pendleton and J. C. Hasler). Academic Press, London.

Freeman, J. and Byrne, P.S. (1976). The assessment of vocational training for general practice. *Report from general practice 17.* Royal College of General Practitioners, London.

—— Roberts, J., Metcalfe, D., and Hillier, V. (1982). *The influence of trainers on trainees in general practice.* Royal College of General Practitioners, London.

The Future General Practitioner (1972). Report of a working party of the Royal College of General Practitioners, London.

Geertsma, R.H. (1969). Studies in self-cognition: an introduction. *J. nerv. ment. dis.* **148**, 193–7.

Hampton, J.R., Harrison, M.J.E., Mitchell, J.R.A., Pritchard, J.S., and Seymour, C. (1975). Relative contributions of history taking, physical examination and laboratory investigation to diagnosis and management of medical outpatients. *Br. med. J.* **ii**, 486–9.

Hannay, D.R. (1979). *The symptom iceberg.* Routledge and Kegan Paul, London.

Hasler, J.C. (1978). Training practices in the Oxford Region. *Jl R. Coll. gen. Practrs* **23**, 353–4.

Havelock, C. (1983). Cervical cytology in general practice. Paper presented at Annual Spring Meeting of the Royal College of General Practitioners, London.

Helfer, R.E. (1970). An objective comparison of the pediatric interviewing skills of freshmen and senior medical students. *Pediatrics* **45**, 623–7.

Helman, C.G. (1981). Diseases versus illness in general practice. *Jl R. Coll. gen. Practrs* **31**, 548–52.

Hornsby, J.L. and Kerr, R.M. (1979). Behavioural science and family practice: a status report. *J. family Pract.* **8**, 299–304.

Hull, F.M. (1980). Time and the general practitioner. *Update* **20**, 435–40.

Illich, I. (1977). *Limits to medicine.* Penguin, Harmondsworth.

Jason, H., Kagan, N., Werner, A., Elstein, A.S., and Thomas, J.B. (1971). New approaches to teaching basic interview skills to medical students. *Am. J. Psychiat.* **127**, 140–3.

Kagan, N., Schauble, P., Resnikoff, A., Danish, S.J., and Krathwohl, D.R. (1969). Interpersonal process recall. *J. nerv. ment. Dis.* **148**, 365–74.

Kahn, G., Cohen, B., and Jason, H. (1979). Teaching interpersonal skills in family practice: results of a national survey. *J. family Pract.* **8**, 309–16.

Kasl, S.V. (1974). The health belief model and behaviour related to chronic illness. *Health Education Monographs* **2**, 433–54.

King, J.B. (1982). Attributions, health beliefs and health behaviour. Doctoral dissertation, University of Oxford.

Kleinman, A. (1980). *Patients and healers in the context of culture.* University of California Press, Berkeley.

Korsch, B.M., Freemon, B., and Negrete, V.F. (1971). Practical implications of doctor–patient interaction: analysis for pediatric practice. *Am. J. Dis. Child.* **121**, 110–14.

Ley, P. (1974). Communications in the clinical setting. *Br. J. Orthodont.* **1**, 173–7.

—— (1976). Towards better doctor–patient communications. In *Communications between doctors and patients* (ed. A. E. Bennett). Oxford University Press for Nuffield Provincial Hospitals Trust.

—— (1977). Psychological studies in doctor–patient communication. In *Contributions to medical psychology* Vol. 1, (ed. S. Rachman). Pergamon, Oxford.

—— (1983). Patients' understanding and recall in clinical communication failure. In *Doctor–patient communication* (ed. D. Pendleton and J. Hasler). Academic Press, London.

McWhinney, I.R. (1972). Beyond diagnosis: an approach to the integration of clinical medicine and behavioural science. *New Engl. J. Med.* **287**, 384–7.

—— (1981). *An introduction to family medicine.* Oxford University Press.

Maddox, H. (1963). *How to study.* Pan, London.

Maguire, G.P., Roe, P., Goldberg, D., Jones, S., Hyde, C., and O'Dowd, T. (1978). The value of feedback in teaching interviewing skills in medical students. *Psychol. Med.* **8**, 695–704.

—— and Rutter, D.R. (1976). History-taking for medical students: 1. Deficiencies in performance. *Lancet* **ii**, 556–8.

Marks, J.N., Goldberg, D.P., and Hillier, V. (1979). Determinants of the ability of general practitioners to detect psychiatric illness. *Pschol. Med.* **9**, 337–53.

Marinker, M. (1981). 2010. *Jl R. Coll. gen. Practrs* **31**, 540–7.

Meadow, R. and Hewitt, C. (1972). Teaching communication skills with the help of actresses and video-tape simulation. *Br. J. med. Education* **6**, 317–22.

Mechanic, D. (1970). Correlates of frustration among British general practitioners. *J. Hlth soc. Behav.* **11**, 87–104.

Melville, A. (1980). Job satisfaction in general practice: implications for prescribing. *Social Sci. Med.* **14a**, 495–9.

Metcalfe, D. (1982). Flexible doctoring. *The Health Services* No. 23, p. 20.

Milligan, J.M. and Stewart, T.I. (1981). The two-way mirror. *Trainee Update* **1**, 116–18.

Osmond, H. (1980). God and the doctor. *New Engl. J. Med.* **302**, 555–8.

Pendleton, D.A. (1981). Doctor–patient communication. Doctoral dissertation, University of Oxford.

—— (1983). Doctor–patient communication: a review. In *Doctor–patient communication* (ed. D. A. Pendleton and J. C. Hasler). Academic Press, London.

—— and Bochner, S. (1980). The communication of medical information in general practice consultations as a function of patients' social class. *Social Sci. Med.* **14a**, 669–73.

—— Brouwer, H., and Jaspars, J. (1983). Communication difficulties: the doctor's perspective. *J. Lang. social Psychol.* **2**, 17–36.

—— and Furnham, A.F. (1980). Skills: a paradigm for applied social psychological research. In *The analysis of social skill* (ed. W. T. Singleton, P. Spurgeon, and R. B. Stammers) pp. 241–55. Plenum, New York.

—— and Schofield, T.P.C. (1983). Motivation and performance in general practice. In *The medical annual* (ed. D. J. Pereira Gray). Wright, Bristol.

—— and Tate, P.H.L. (1981). *Consulting in general practice: a 4 part video series.* MSD Foundation, London.

—— and Wakeford, R.E. (1979). Training in interpersonal skills for medical students: an evaluation study. Paper presented at the Scientific Meeting of the Association for the Study of Medical Education, University of Southampton.

Pennebaker, J.W. and Skelton, J.A. (1981). Psychological parameters of physical symptoms. *Personality social Psychol. Bull.* **4**, 524–30.

Pietroni, P. (1976). Non-verbal communication in the general practice surgery. In *Language and communication in general practice* (ed. B. Tanner). Hodder and Stoughton, London.

Podell, R.N. (1975). *Physician's guide to compliance in hypertension.* Merck, Pennsylvania.

Raynes, N.V. (1980). A preliminary study of search procedures and patient management techniques in general practice. *Jl. R. Coll. Gen. Practrs.* **13**, 166–72.

Royal College of General Practitioners (1975). Tape recording consultations. (Editorial.) *Jl R. Coll. gen. Practrs* **159**, 705–6.

—— (1981*a*). *Health and prevention in primary care. Occasional Paper 18.* London.

—— (1981*b*). *Prevention of arterial disease in general practice. Occasional Paper 19.* London.

—— (1981*c*). *What sort of doctor?* London.

Rosenstock, I.M. (1966). Why people use health services. *Millbank Memorial Fund Quarterly* **44**, 94–127.

Rotter, J. (1966). Generalized expectancies for internal vs. external control of reinforcement. *Psychol. Monogr.* **80**, no. 609.

Russell, M.A.H., Wilson, C., Taylor, C., and Baker, C.D. (1979). Effect of general practitioners' advice against smoking. *Br. med. J.* **ii**, 231–5.

Rutter, D.R. and Maguire, G.P. (1976). History taking for medical students: 2: Evaluation of a training programme. *Lancet* **ii**, 558–60.

Sackett, D.L. and Haynes, R.B. (eds.) (1976). *Compliance with therapeutic regimens.* Johns Hopkins University Press, Baltimore.

Stott, N.C.H. and Davis, R.H. (1979). The exceptional potential in each primary care consultation. *Jl R. Coll. gen. Practrs* **29**, 201–5.

Tait, I.E. (1977). The clinical record in British general practice. *Br. med. J.* **ii**, 683–8.

Tate, P. (in presentation). The problems presented to a general practitioner.

Taylor, (1977). Television in general practice. *Update* **15**, 489–94.

Tuckett, D. (ed.) (1976). *An introduction to medical sociology.* Tavistock, London.

—— (1982). *Final report on the patient project.* Health Education Council, London.

Verby, J.E., Holden, P., and Davis, R.H. (1979). Peer review of consultations in primary care: the use of audio visual recordings. *Br. med. J.* **i**, 1686–8.

Waitzkin, H. and Stoeckle, J.D. (1972). The communication of information about illness: clinical, social and methodological considerations. *Adv. psychosomat. Med.* **8**, 180–215.

—— —— (1976). Information control and the micropolitics of health care: summary of an on-going research project. *Social Sci. Med.* **10**, 263–76.

Wakeford, R. (1983). Communication skills training in United Kingdom medical schools. In *Doctor–patient communication* (ed. D. A. Pendleton and J. C. Hasler). Academic Press, London.

Wallston, B.S. and Wallston, K.A. (1978). Locus of control and health: a review of the literature. *Hlth Education Monogr.* **6**, 107–17.

Wallston, K.A., Wallston, B.S., and De Vellis, R. (1978). Development of the multi-dimensional health locus of control (MHLC) scales. *Hlth Education Monogr.* **6**, 160–9.

Weed, L.L. (1968). Medical records that guide and teach. *New Engl. J. Med.* **278**, 593.

Zander, L.I. (1978). *Medical records in general practice.* Royal College of General Practitioners, London.

Zigmond, D. (1978). When Balinting is mind rape. *Update* **6**, 1123–7.

Zola, I.K. (1972). Studying the decision to see a doctor: review, critique, corrective. In *Psychosocial aspects of physical illness. Advances in Psychosomatic Medicine, Vol 8* (ed. Z. J. Lipowski). Karger, Basle.

—— (1973). Pathways to the doctor – from person to patient. *Social Sci. Med.* **7**, 677–89.

Index